PAVILION TO CREASE
... AND BACK

Mark Wagh

photographs by Sam Bowles

foreword by Stephen Fleming

FAIRFIELD BOOKS

Fairfield Books
17 George's Road, Fairfield Park, Bath BA1 6EY
Tel 01225-335813

Cover design by Rob Taylor
Cover image by Sam Bowles

First published 2009

ISBN: 978 0 9560702 3 4

Printed and bound in Great Britain by
Midway Colour Print, Holt, Wiltshire

Contents

Foreword by Stephen Fleming

When I was asked by Mark Wagh to write a foreword to the book he had just written, I did wonder if I would be suitably qualified. Would I be able to provide an entrée that would compliment the thesis or theories of one of the more intelligent men to have played the great game of cricket? After reading the book I am honoured to be contributing.

This is an excellent recount of a county season. It is accurate and honest and gives you an idea of the work, both mental and physical, that goes into playing a full county season. It also offers an insight into the fears and anxieties that are a dismissal away from dominating your every thought. The fact that the 'fear of failure' can be the catalyst for performance indicates the volatile nature of a cricketer's mind. It is why Test cricket is called what it is!

I don't usually read about cricket, but I really did enjoy this book. And it helped jog the memories from my time at Trent Bridge. They were some of my most enjoyable days of cricket with a great group of guys, a smart manager and a great ground.

2007, the year Mark joined us, was an interesting season. The year before, we had gone from defending champions to cellar dwellers with an embarrassing finish, being convincingly beaten by eventual winners Sussex. We only needed three points from the game to avoid being relegated, and we were lucky to get two. It was hard to accept that things could turn so quickly, and I vowed that afternoon, as I watched Sussex take our title, to return next year hell bent on getting us back into Division One.

To do this we would need some reinforcements, and the coach Mick Newell set about building a team that could not only get us back into the top echelon but could seriously challenge the top teams in the country. When he told me we had signed Mark Waugh, I was delighted. The former Australian great would be a fantastic addition, even if he had been out of the game for a couple of years.

"No," Mick replied. "It's Mark Wagh from Birmingham."

"Oh ... um ... wow ... that's great!"

In all seriousness, it was an excellent signing. Mark was a good player who maybe needed a change of scenery to see how good he could be. He had been at Warwickshire for many years and was at risk of becoming comfortable – not that the environment at Edgbaston sounded anything like comfortable, but it would have provided familiarity and routine. The time was right!

My first substantial encounter with Waggy was when I arrived back into the Notts changing rooms, fashionably late due to New Zealand commitments and an overdue marriage. I was surprised to see our new recruit already well-entrenched, sitting proudly next to the 'Sapper' Ealham. He was sitting with a beaming smile radiating my way. In that beautiful moment I couldn't help but think how much he reminded me of Jah Jah Binks, the loveable creature from *Star Wars*! That smile was gradually sapped as Ealy and coach Newell went to work.

The thing that struck me when watching my new team-mate bat for the first time was his excellent defence. Most players at this level can play a cover drive or a flick off the legs, but not all value the ability to stay at the wicket when things aren't that easy. Mark has all the shots, don't get me wrong. He is elegant when driving and surprisingly adept at pulling and hooking which can be difficult for taller players, but he almost gets better when challenged by a good bowler or a sporting wicket.

Reading this book, I took immense pride in Waggy's inability to convert 50s into 100s. This was my Achilles' heel, and I'm delighted that Mark has taken something from my time playing with him!

I loved my time with Notts. We did the full circle in the three years I was there: a championship win to the despair of being relegated to the joy of scrapping hard and earning promotion. To read how close Notts came to winning another championship after being promoted was entertaining and real. It's also great to read how coach Newell and Mark have become so close; they take a love-hate relationship to new levels. I remember a line Mick said to me when Waggy was walking back to the rooms after another 'soft' dismissal: "For a smart man, he plays dumb cricket!"

Introduction

I am a professional cricketer. A batsman. My value to the team is measured by the number of runs I score. It is a fragile career, success and failure often separated by the gossamer of fortune. There are few certainties but I can be sure of one journey. I will leave the changing rooms and walk out onto the cricket field. I will carry with me the hopes and expectations of my team-mates and supporters. And I will return, sometimes a hero, sometimes a villain. I will do this 30 or 40 times a season. Always the same journey, but never the same story. From pavilion to crease … and back.

This is the story of my year: one of the most emotionally charged of my career. It is not a misty-eyed, fairy tale where the hero overcomes initial adversity to triumph in the end. I warn you: there are more lows than highs in this book.

It is the story of a cricket team whose initial aim was simply to avoid relegation but which came within a whisker of winning the Championship and one ball away from winning the Pro40 league.

I've tried to portray the events as they happened, writing in real time without the benefit of hindsight. I had no real idea where the diary would end up, what it would contain, indeed whether it would ever see the light of day. I wanted to produce something that was a fair reflection of what went on, how I felt and my reactions to events. Not a saccharine-coated homage to professional sport.

The passing of a year is often measured by the changing of the seasons. This ebb and flow of nature is also mirrored in a county cricketer's activity. He starts in the depths of winter in the indoor school, then he emerges into the first optimistic light of spring, basks in the full height of the summer and finally experiences culmination, celebrated, confetti-like, by the first falling leaves of autumn. To stretch the analogy a little further, the dynamics of the team also fluctuate with the changing climate: from disparate nomadic individuals during the cold winter months, then a coming together during pre-season, joy in summer and often a slight staleness in autumn. It's a process with which I suspect that most cricketers throughout the ages can identify. After all, sport is just one manifestation of the human condition, and that hasn't changed too much over the last few years.

Of course some things have changed: the number of matches, the design of the competitions, and the physical make-up of the participants. We play several formats of the game, creating a high volume of cricket during the year. In the days of single-division cricket, there was a lot of meandering: playing games which probably wouldn't impact on the title

race. Even over the period of my career I've noticed an increase in the value placed on each and every result.

I hope this book will give you an insight into the world of a modern county cricketer: from the technicalities of performance to the drama provided by the sport. So, with the umpires walking out to the middle, it's time to get started …

Chapter One

2006 … 2007 …

This is my second year at Notts after eight years at Warwickshire. The decision to leave Edgbaston at the end of 2006 crystallised during a stay in India. I was sitting in my aunt and uncle's apartment in Mumbai, and I could hardly recognise the person I remembered from the summer. He had dreaded going through the large blue gates at Edgbaston. He had lost any sense of enjoyment from cricket and become dispirited, cynical and sad. Yet at the time it didn't feel like that. Sure, I was on the wrong side of the coach's opinion, but I was in the team nevertheless, and life shouldn't be too easy, should it?

Edgbaston was full of people who, even if they hadn't been my team-mates, I would have been happy to call my friends. Yet something within me during 2006 had stopped me from fully engaging with them. I think it was that my disillusionment with the environment had seeped into my psyche. It took time and distance, though, for that realisation.

2006 had provided a 'perfect storm' of personal factors: I had split from my fiancée, I considered giving up the game for the first time in my life, and I turned 30. For most of the summer I was wishing away time, something I had promised myself I would never do. Yet there I was, looking towards the end of September as some kind of salvation; I wouldn't have to endure the day-to-day grinding effect of being at Warwickshire. As I've said, this wasn't something that was evident to me at the time, as a kind of helpless acceptance had imperceptibly enveloped me. It wasn't as though every day was gloom and despondency, but there was an ease with which I assumed these states. I had developed an outlook based around fear: fear of failure, fear of upsetting management, fear of the future. It was enervating to foresee a positive outcome on the field. The idea of doing well was something that took too much effort at times, and it's hard to enjoy something when the overwhelming emotion associated with it is dread.

The decision to leave Warwickshire, the county I had played for since I was 10, was something that evolved. Reading through the previous paragraph, you might think that it was a straightforward decision. But I had had many good times at the club and, having been there for so long, it felt like a marriage – you work through the tough issues, you don't walk away from them.

I had gone through lists of pros and cons ad nauseam but, sitting there in Mumbai in late October, it occurred to me that I was trying to find reasons to stay and that the most obvious path, to a new county, was just that – obvious and therefore correct. The cloak that had dulled me, through which the world seemed grey and uninviting, had already started to lift, and this decision was something I suddenly realised had been made for a while, as though someone had been sitting next to me and I had only just noticed. I felt a new kind of optimism and lightness, one that didn't need any effort. I was becoming more comfortable and accepting of myself. A version of myself that I actually liked was emerging – and it felt fantastic.

Fast forward to March 2007. I had been away travelling in the intervening time, taking in Buenos Aires, New York, Chicago and Sydney. I needed that time to rid myself of the destructive vestiges of the previous couple of years. Now, walking up the stairs to the home changing rooms at Trent Bridge, I felt optimistic and energised but, as I heard the voices and laughter, I felt a little nervous. On the other side of the door was a group of guys reacquainting themselves with team-mates they hadn't seen over the winter, and I was a newcomer entering their environment.

As I opened the door and walked through, there was a slight pause as everyone looked up. After a couple of "hellos" and "all rights?" I heard "Over here, sweetheart, come and sit next to me." It was Mark Ealham. I subsequently realised that he calls everyone sweetheart (fortunately!). I dropped my bags down and started chatting. Pretty quickly I realised I was going to enjoy being amongst these guys.

I was understandably keen to assure my team-mates I wasn't a 'dud', but my pre-season form was very average. When you come into a team as a new player, you assume a certain level in the hierarchy. The fact that the coach has actively sought your services means that you start in his favour. You are probably taking someone's place in the team. And this has been achieved without doing anything for the club itself. So it can lead to some resentment if others feel that that level of goodwill isn't justified.

However, from the first innings against Leicester (70), I felt comfortable and quickly settled into a routine of scoring 50s, 60s and 70s without converting them into anything particularly substantial. There is a feeling which all sportsmen suffer from that, whatever one achieves, it is not quite good enough. It motivates, and retaining an ever-rising ceiling allows for limitless achievement; at least that's how the theory goes. Well, just between you and me, I think that a modicum of satisfaction, not endless gloating of course, is good for the soul. I would have loved to have accumulated bigger scores, but my method didn't change when I reached a half-century, and it was good enough to get me there in the first place, so I took the view that, if they weren't meant to be, then so be it. Nevertheless I managed to finish as the club's highest run-scorer in both championship and one-day cricket and we were promoted to Division

One. Picking up the club's Player of the Year award was, I feel, a moment of justifiable satisfaction.

There were a few reasons for my good form last year, primarily based around a good dollop of happiness. The environment which coach Mick Newell has created is one of relaxed joviality, mixed with a high degree of expectation. Having been on the receiving end of one of his 'blasts', when he felt I hadn't performed to the appropriate level, there was no need for further reminders or hints about complacency. There was also a pleasing assumption that we were keen to be the best we could be and didn't enjoy losing. In my experience, coaches do not always make that assumption.

Management sometimes assume that no-one is more motivated to win than themselves and, left to our own devices, we players would allow any talent we had to wither, snuffed out by a lack of training or desire. I've sat through countless post-defeat meetings when the coach or captain expresses how much it hurt them to lose whilst questioning the impact on the rest of us.

I was also lucky enough to work with Jamil Qureshi. His expertise and friendship were crucial ingredients in changing my outlook from one of fear to one of expectation. Jamil's background (cricketer turned stand-up comic turned magician turned psychologist) meant that he approached the issue of sports psychology from a unique angle. Sessions included hypnosis, suggestion techniques based on neuro-linguistic programming and lessons he had learned from working with the world's top golfers and many successful corporations.

The promotion to Division One of the Championship was crucial. There is undoubtedly a difference in standard between the two divisions: there are probably four or five considerably weaker teams in the second division whereas in the first there are usually only one or two at most. There's virtually no let-up in quality so runs and wickets are worth more.

Something fundamental changed in my outlook during 2007. Throughout my career, playing for England had never been far from my thoughts. During the winters it would prompt me to train on those days when I felt cold, tired or fed up, and in the summer months I always viewed good or bad form through the prism of England ambitions. I'm sure that I was no different from a lot of my fellow cricketers. But, as I had turned thirty, I realised that the chances of fulfilling my dream were remote. Letting go was a release. No longer constrained by this need, and feeling that I had yet to achieve all that I could, I took on the role of an interested bystander. With the object of interest being me.

I wanted to see how good I could be. Perhaps in the next five years I would average 50 or 60 or 70. Who knows? All I knew was what I had done to that point suggested that I could play a little. Occasionally I played really well, other times I could be more amateur than professional. There is always that element of doubt when you walk to the crease: will I see the first few balls? will my feet move? will I get off the mark? Now, instead of worrying about this, I became curious as to how I would react. He's bowling fast and swinging it? Great, let's see if I can cope. I would never discover the extent of my ability if I only performed when it was easy and feared those times when it wasn't.

And in 2007 I did surprise myself. I played shots I didn't realise I could; I survived in conditions I didn't think I would; and I succeeded when doubts were racing through my head. I remember a Pro40 game against Sussex at Hove towards the end of the season. It was the start of the innings. Chris Liddle, a left-arm seamer, bowled a widish ball across me which I tried to drive but only managed to play and miss. The slips and keeper voiced their pleasure with my shot. Now, in the past I would have remonstrated with myself, replaying what I should have done, trying consciously to improve my response to the ball. But this time I figuratively shrugged my shoulders: I trusted my instincts, and they clearly felt I could have hit it. The next ball was almost identical. There's no way for me to prove this, but I would say in every other year of my career I would have left it, having played and missed at the previous ball. Instead, I drove it through extra cover for four. A great example of surprising myself by trusting my instincts.

One of the reasons I've heard that I haven't played for England is that I'm not considered mentally strong. It's a tough term to define, but it generally refers to the ability to block out extraneous factors and concentrate on the job at hand. These factors may include previous form, criticism, poor conditions, indeed virtually anything that can be used as an excuse (justifiably or not) for a bad performance.

Of course, every success involves a degree of mental strength as there are always factors we are trying to overcome. In succeeding, we have 'blocked out' their malign influence and focused on the job. So I suppose my critics were saying I wasn't mentally strong *enough*.

At Warwickshire Nick Knight seemed to think I could only perform on flat wickets. When conditions were a little tough, either a technical failure or a mental weakness would let me down. So I guess he must have been a little surprised that I scored as many runs as I did at Trent Bridge, given the bowler-friendly nature of the ground. But maybe he'll be proved right this year?

The charge of mental weakness is difficult to defend. As far as I know, there is no empirical measure so it comes down to inference and anecdote. I can certainly think of countless examples of times when I have demonstrated mental strength, but then I would say that, wouldn't I?

The reason I haven't played for England is that I haven't scored enough runs to make my selection unavoidable. When a group of players are all scoring a similar amount of runs, there needs to be some way to differentiate between them. Character is often the arbiter and rightly so. After all, the selectors are in the business of prediction, never an exact science. Success at any level is a result of talent and character.

What rankles, though, is the ease with which I have been labelled: a single line that has put paid to a lifetime's ambition. How can someone know if I would be mentally strong enough to succeed at international level? My response to that environment would be unknown to everyone, including me. The fact that I have scored 10,000 first-class runs at an average of 40, predominately on a ground not renowned for heavy scoring, should be testament to a degree of talent and mental ability.

Each cricket club is a unique set of people, facilities and environment. The contrast between my former club and Notts was stark. The changing rooms are a good way to illustrate this. At Warwickshire, we had just moved into a vast space beneath the RV Ryder Stand. It was a pretty impersonal space, big and devoid of a view of the ground. But, given the large staff (over thirty cricketers at various times), we needed a big area to accommodate everyone. Contrast this to the compact, intimate changing area at Trent Bridge. A smaller staff, a warmer feel.

The greatest difference, though, was in the coach. Mark Greatbatch came to Edgbaston in controversial circumstances. The appointing panel was split between him and the other candidate, Andy Moles. Unbelievably, there was no agreed protocol should the four-man panel be split. The subsequent wrangling led to the resignation of the Chairman of Cricket, Tim Munton.

The club realised they had made a mistake with Mark but only after two years of his three-year contract. As a batting coach, the only contribution I saw him make was to lay a piece of string from one end to the other as a guide for which balls to leave alone. From what I understand, this was more than he offered the bowlers. He gave me no advice as to strategy in any form of the game. His man-management skills, as I experienced them, were awful.

As an example, in his first year, I discovered I wasn't playing in the first game of season only when he read the team out to the whole group. No explanation or forewarning. Apparently he had become concerned during pre-season with something in my game. But rather than tell me then, and help, he just left me out of the first game.

There was one area in which he and Mick Newell, the Notts coach, are similar: persona during a game. Both become stressed and difficult to be around. But, whereas Mark remained unapproachable after the game, Mick quickly returns to his normal reasonable self and allows himself to be part of the dressing-room banter.

My feelings about my time at Edgbaston are tinged with regret. I look back to unfulfilled promise and to battling to be accepted for who I was. I feel an impulsive instinct to hedge what I've just said, so take it as read that there were counterbalancing times too. It's difficult to give a fair, rounded reflection as the last year or so is foremost in my mind, casting a malevolent shadow over memories of earlier happier times.

One of the things I'm most proud of is my opening partnership at Warwickshire with Nick Knight. Nick was a phenomenal producer of runs: his method at times looked ropey, at other times he played beautifully. But how he was playing was almost irrelevant because he always churned out scores. Opening with him was an honour, and I was particularly happy to be the one walking out with him for his final first-class innings in September 2006. We were close friends – though, when he took over the captaincy, we became less so, perhaps as a natural result of his position. I felt less able to laugh about things with him. But the fact that I was Nick Knight's opening partner for a time gives me great satisfaction.

From an excellent left-hander to a great – Brian Lara. I was extremely lucky to play half a summer with Brian in 1998 after I came back from Oxford. My first game was at Edgbaston. We had won the toss and were batting. It was about 10.45 a.m., and I was having some last minute throwdowns from Phil Neale who was a touch distracted – Brian had yet to turn up and hadn't been contactable. Just as we were packing up, he drove into the ground in his bright yellow Peugeot sports car, unfazed, unhurried and oblivious to the whirlpool of stress to which he had reduced the coach.

We batted together in a game at Worcester. I had opened the batting and had just completed my first hundred for the county when Brian came to the wicket. He had faced about a dozen balls when I realised that it would not be long before he was overtaking me. Each over he would hit two or three fours and then steer the ball towards one of the deep fielders and stroll through for a single, leaving me one ball (which Brian clearly viewed as a chance to rest his weary legs on his bat and watch – there was very little danger of a quick single at this stage).

One over from left-arm spinner Richard Illingworth sticks in my mind. Brian smashed the first ball over long on for four, prompting the fielder to drop out. He then swept the next ball hard in front of square for another boundary. Deep backward square duly moved round a little. The third ball disappeared over deep mid-wicket as Brian picked the gap perfectly between the recently repositioned fielders. This led to the slip coming out to mid-wicket and the fielder there dropping back onto the boundary. The fourth ball I can still picture as if it was happening now. Richard tried to spear the ball into the stumps with as much pace as possible. As I watched the ball travel down towards Brian, his bat seemed suspended high in the air as the ball honed in on the stumps. Just when I thought it was too late, he brought his bat down with ferocious speed and back-cut the ball through the vacant slip area. Needless to say, the fifth ball was a single!

I was also fortunate to be at the club when Bob Woolmer returned for a second stint. In so many ways Bob was a brilliant coach: his innovation, fresh thinking and passion for cricket have been well documented. When it was announced that he was to take over from Phil Neale, I and a couple of others went out to Cape Town for a three-week period before the rest of the squad came across for the pre-season tour.

I was desperate to experience what I'd heard so much about; I was straining at the leash to meet him. Unfortunately we barely saw him as his other commitments only left room for a handful of net sessions. However, we did have a BBQ, or braai, at his house which was the highlight of the trip. In his study, lined with Wisdens and cricket videos, we chatted about the game and his enthusiasm was infectious. He wanted to improve every area, refusing to be limited by convention.

I don't think Bob was prepared for the politics of the club, and his enthusiasm quickly waned. We won promotion into Division One despite some inconsistent performances. But we weren't improving as a team, and I don't think Bob's heart was really in the job.

But I will always remember the day he presented me with my county cap at Chelmsford. Almost from the first time I walked into the Indoor School at Edgbaston, seeing the pictures on the wall of the capped players, I dreamt of earning one myself. I did a Sky interview after that day's play, and Charles Colville mentioned I was looking particularly pleased. I could barely take the smile off my face.

I was always a little frustrated that Warwickshire wasn't the best club in the country: It had the financial clout, fantastic facilities, ambition and a central location in a big city. It should have attracted and kept any player it wanted. But it seemed that it always fudged issues, trying to resolve things whilst keeping everyone happy and never confronting them head on. This wasn't helped by a myriad of people having a say – committee, officials and management. With so many agendas, it became a political monstrosity with personal conflict, rumour mongering, territorial disputes and back stabbing. There was also an air of hubris, the club assuming that it was *the* choice destination, only to discover in fact it wasn't. Any success the club enjoyed was despite rather than because of its best efforts.

What about the players? Well, with a large playing staff there was plenty of peering over one's shoulder – and, with a large coaching structure, there were plenty of opinions flying around about our playing abilities, with personality issues feeding into this slightly insecure environment. It was a political entity, both front and back stage.

I feel I should hedge again. This is only my opinion, my take on how I experienced the club. Speak to others, and you'll probably get a different view. I always think of Nick Knight on issues like this because he had a diametrically opposed view to mine. I am slightly reluctant to hypothesise how he would argue on this point as he clearly can't have a come back here. So, with appropriate caution, I would suggest he would refuse to accept any indictment of environment, especially if I claimed that it could have affected performance. He would probably say that it was personal weakness to blame external factors for any poor performance. He's right, but he experienced something very different to me; he received star treatment, and he never had to worry about his name not appearing on the team sheet. This was, of course, because of his exceptional record.

Who's right? Both of us probably. Rarely is something all good or all bad; it's usually a frustrating mixture of the two. We just saw different sides of the same coin.

Chapter Two

January and February

Friday 11 January

Today is what most cricketers dread – fitness testing. Bleep tests, strength tests, sprints and a panoply of instruments designed to differentiate muscle from fat are all produced from the evil fitness coach's bag of tricks. Fortunately, this time it was a relatively relaxed affair, and it was fun to catch up with the guys and hear about what they have been up to. I also had my first net session with the batting coach, Paul Johnson. He spent his entire career at Nottingham and keenly feels every win or loss. He's an excellent batting coach, focusing on what can be achieved, shots to play, rather than worrying about getting out. But most importantly I tend to trust his judgment.

There is an unspoken fear before this inaugural session of the new campaign, probably felt by every batsman since the game began, that "I've lost it," it being the ability to hit a ball. I did see this happen to one person when I was growing up, and it has remained a source of much pre-season concern. So, when I managed to get the bat in the way of the first ball, I felt like popping the champagne.

Monday 14 January

I've spent the day with Mick Newell, Chris Read and five others (nominally the senior players, although that makes us a fairly senior-laden team) chatting through management issues with Michael Fordham from the Bradford School of Management. We spoke about the decision-making process within a group, the attribution of blame, and dealing with success and failure. I quite enjoyed it. I often feel these issues are swamped by cliché and a degree of playing to audience – saying things the coach or captain wants to hear. This however was refreshingly honest: it's one of the reasons I like Notts so much. Mick is a good coach because he encourages candidness; he doesn't just pay lip service to others' opinions but listens to the results. It takes a certain confidence to open yourself up to potential criticism from those below, and it seems to be a reasonable rule of thumb that a willingness to do so is directly proportional to ability to do the job.

One thing did worry me slightly. When Mick and Chris spoke of hopes for this coming season, after the usual pre-season pleasantries, they said finishing mid-table would be a good result. It worries me because behind great achievements there is often inspirational confidence. Nick Knight's absolute belief in our method as a team was the foundation of

Warwickshire's Championship winning season in 2004. In moments when the team is unsure, we will need someone who can communicate their confidence that we will prevail. But it has to be a genuine belief. Nick did this and, after a few instances of his being proved correct, we all started believing too. Cricket is full of uncertainties, the margins so narrow, that belief really can transmute into reality. If they're assuming we will win some, lose some, it will be difficult to be convincing when the tide of expectation is turning against us.

I'm not sure how, or even if, I'm going to broach this with Mick. I realise that this runs contrary to what I've just said, but I think I'd feel uncomfortable mentioning it, primarily because part of me actually agrees with them: it is a competitive league, relegation is indeed a possibility. It's also very easy to pontificate from the sidelines, and I doubt I would have the conviction I'm suggesting they should have. But I do think a component of leadership is to be bold, to help people see past any fears that they may have in the moment. Ultimately, though, it will be deeds not words that will matter. In that I take heart because Chris is someone whose example will be inspirational.

Tuesday 15 January
I've received some good news. I've been asked to go on an MCC tour to Uganda in February, all expenses paid for three weeks. Needless to say, I have jumped at the chance.

Wednesday 30 January
Training is going well. I've been putting time in at the gym, and my weekly net against the bowling machine has left me feeling good about my game. Of course, it would be slightly worrying if, in a situation in which I know where the ball is going to pitch, I didn't play it well, but nevertheless I think I'm progressing nicely.

I'm in the process of selling my house in Birmingham and moving up to Nottingham; I hadn't realised quite how stressful the procedure is. There are five people in my chain. There are so many things that need to happen at the right time, an endless list of things that can go wrong. I'm desperate to move before I go to Uganda which ups the pressure a little more.

It seems odd to me, given my job involves being under pressure, that the current situation is producing such a reaction in me. I guess it's partly to do with the helplessness I feel in relation to organising other people. If only I could make some calls, hurry people along further down the chain...

By the next instalment, I shall either be tremendously relieved or too stressed for words.

Friday 8 February

It is with some satisfaction that I am writing this. The computer is sitting on a desk (assembled by yours truly), in a study without a box in sight, in a house which now contains all my furniture and belongings in approximately the appropriate places. Moving in has been virtually stress-free (I realise that I'm tempting the Fates, but I'm hoping they aren't keen readers), despite the boxes having something of the rabbit about them and seemingly multiplying overnight: just when I thought I'd dealt with them all, another couple appear in a corner.

I have absolutely no DIY skills. In the past, it has taken me over eight hours to put together an Ikea desk (so now you can see why I'm so satisfied); picture hanging is probably the limit of my abilities, and even in that I wouldn't trust myself. So Mike Cheshire is a godsend. He is a man with apparently unlimited aptitude around the house and without him I would be completely lost.

My thoughts for the last couple of weeks have revolved around the house sale. I'm delighted that I'm in my new home and especially happy that I haven't had to deal with this when cricket starts. I can now turn my attention to this coming season and, for almost the first time, start preparing for Uganda.

Tuesday 12 February

I mentioned in my last post that I could now focus on cricket. The truth of the matter is that I've barely given it a second thought. This past week has seen me running around, arranging workmen, furniture and curtains – the most nightmarish, stressful process for any item I have ever attempted to buy. It's like being forced to solve Fermat's last theorem with GCSE maths: too many variables, no skill to make any sense of them, and the certainty that I will make a terrible mistake.

However, now that I'm sitting on the train down to London, bags packed, passport safely lodged and camera ready, I feel that cricket is firmly on the agenda. The weather helps: glorious, spirit-lifting blue skies and just warm enough to think about training outdoors.

I feel quite excited. It's cricket starting again, there's a group of people to get to know, and Uganda is a complete unknown to me. I watched the *Last King of Scotland* on DVD over the weekend as an introduction to the country but will try to pick up a guide book at the airport. I like the idea of discovering a new part of the world. I read about a cyclist who was riding around the world in 180 days, covering 100 miles a day. That kind of adventure always appeals to me, but I lack the gumption to do anything about it. Perhaps next year …

Thursday 14 February

MCC 202 for nine (50 overs, Peploe 50, Wagh 3)
Uganda under-19 117 all out
MCC won by 85 runs

Valentine's Day has left a mark on my heart, unfortunately it's a bruise from a ball that took off from a length. The delivery that scuttled along the deck shortly after and accounted for my leg stump, ensured that my first game of the tour was not a personally profitable one. Fortunately we won the game relatively easily, although the standard of the pitch is an ominous sign.

The tour party consists of a mixture of professionals (Jamie Dalrymple and Dave Harrison from Glamorgan; Ben Scott and Chris Peploe from Middlesex; and me and Billy Shafayat from Notts), minor counties players and very good club players. The aim of these trips is to promote the game in countries where cricket is developing and could benefit from the presence and experience of a group such as ours.

I'm sure our manager, Steve Salisbury, is particularly happy with the win, given what happened last night. Steve is a teacher at the Duke of York's Royal Military School and is the walking personification of all that is good about the MCC. He is fiercely keen to win but would never consider infringing upon the spirit of the game to do so. He is a man who will perform his duty to the club with his dying breath. And he has never, as far as I am aware, ever declined a 'club spirit' – a double gin and tonic.

Back to last night. We were hosted by the Ugandan Cricket Board. A succession of dignitaries made various welcoming speeches, and Steve spoke excellently about our pleasure to be here and the spirit of cricket, which is a central theme in MCC matches. However the final dignitary decided to change tack from his predecessors and went on an anti-colonial, anti-English rant, telling his players to ignore the spirit of cricket and to win at any cost. I could see Steve's smile slowly fading as the gentleman stumbled from one disconnected theme to the next. At one point he seemed to suggest that Steve was related to Lord Salisbury, the former Prime Minister who supported policies that led to the Boer War – at this point his smile was decidedly strained.

Early impressions of the country: everywhere is lush green, the people are laid back and friendly, and the food is excellent and cheap.

Friday 15 February

MCC 98 all out (Wagh 24) and 95 for one (Wagh 50)*
Uganda under-19 97 all out (Harrison 7-22)

It's funny that, even against this less-than-full-strength opposition, the sense of satisfaction from scoring a few runs is still strong. I'm 50 not out overnight, and the congratulations from my team-mates have ensured that I'm feeling content with my first contribution of the tour. It's a timely reminder of one of the reasons I play the game.

After play, we coached a group of disabled cricketers. Unfortunately some easily treatable causes of disability, such as polio, are still problems here, although incidences are dropping. It's easy to drift into mild condescension, but these guys were tough, resilient people who absolutely loved playing cricket. One man, who had lost both legs, had fashioned a bike powered by his arms and cycled across town to come to these sessions. Given the pot-holes, insane traffic and hilly nature of the roads, this was some feat. Keith Newell, the former Sussex and Glamorgan all-rounder, did a superb job running the session through an interpreter; it really brought home the good sport can do.

Saturday 16 February

MCC 98 all out and 252 for five (Beeny 100*, Wagh 83)
Uganda under-19 97 & 145 all out (Dalrymple 5-33)
MCC won by 108 runs

Sunday 17 February

MCC 173 all out (Wagh 29)
Uganda 175 for seven
MCC lost by three wickets

We faced our first real test yesterday against the full Ugandan team in a 50-over game and lost. As with any one-day defeat it is possible to highlight a multitude of areas in which to lay the blame, but conceding 45 extras as we did was a fairly obvious one.

I'm happy with the way I'm hitting the ball: I am trying to get into the mindset of expecting to score runs every time I go to the wicket. Part of me thinks that I have a finite number of good scores in me, or the luck needed to get those scores, and that I don't want to use it up in less important games. And if I've done well in the last few innings, then I'm definitely due a low score. These self-limiting thought processes seem silly, ludicrous even, when I look at what I've just written, but I guess not every thought is a rational one.

Andy Flower once described batting to me as a mental ordeal. I often think of that when I'm batting as it is so often true. The time between balls and overs allows one's mind to wander, creating problems when none exist, distorting reality. This little bubble of distortion bursts the moment we get out, and the true situation reveals itself and you get the "why did I do that?" moment. For example, during a run chase, a few runless balls can seem catastrophic for the batsmen in the middle but relatively inconsequential to those watching. There are also those images running through my mind's eye. Too often they seem to show me missing straight balls, nicking the ball behind, etc. Jamil has helped me to reinterpret some of the images that pop up in my mind, seeing them as helpful reminders from my subconscious rather than self-sabotaging thoughts.

This afternoon we visited a local orphanage. The kids were great: full of energy, curiosity and smiles. They loved having their picture taken and seeing the results. I have virtually no ability to relate to kids, we may as well be inhabitants from different planets. These events are frustrating for me: I'd love to connect to the children like some of my team-mates did, but I don't know how, I just feel awkward.

Thursday 21 February

I've just returned from drinks at the British High Commission. It seems to be a perk of touring with the MCC that we are treated in ways which I haven't experienced before. The Ugandan team and administration were present, along with a selection of ex-pats and Foreign Office officials. As enjoyable as the evening was, the real fun started when my room-mate Adam Syddall, Steve Salisbury and I got in a taxi to return to the hotel.

The car itself had clearly seen better days, and I had some doubts over its functional capacity as the driver seemed suspiciously reluctant to test out the lights or brakes. The zebra-skin seat covers must have been a tasty addition to the aesthetic back in the 60s when they were clean but unfortunately not now, caked in the grime from the intervening years as they were. As we spluttered towards home, Steve tried to engage in some friendly banter with the cabbie, a laudable yet ultimately hilarious effort since neither party seemed to understand a word the other was saying. On the final hill to the hotel, the asthmatic car finally gave up the ghost. Fortunately a friendly local gave us a lift for the final mile or so. This chap clearly hadn't passed any sort of driving test, judging by the way he crunched his way through the gears despite Steve urging him to show some compassion for the tortured gear box.

Friday 22 February
(3-day game)
Uganda 220 all out
MCC 47 for no wicket (Wagh 38*)

There is a slight unease within the camp. The local press have suggested we sulked off after the one-day defeat and on the field relations are slightly strained. So after play today we shared a crate of beer with the Ugandans in an effort to defuse the situation. I think it worked. They are a talented bunch of highly motivated cricketers, but they sometimes get consumed by the emotion of the moment. Their athleticism in the field has been extraordinary (the outfield is almost corrugated, making fielding pretty difficult, but at times the Ugandans make it look like they are fielding at Lord's).

I'm 38 not out, having struck the ball as well as I have done for a while. I'm excited by the way I played today, and I'd love to take this into the English season. At the moment I wish the season was starting tomorrow.

Monday 25 February
Uganda 220 and 195 for eight, declared
MCC 193 (Shafayat 68*, Wagh 47) and 114 for five (Wagh 18*)
Match drawn

The three-day game fizzled out into a draw, hardly surprising as to win we were set five runs an over on the last day, when the match average was about 2.5.

I'm reading Bill Clinton's autobiography. One of the most striking aspects of the book is the clarity with which Clinton understands his own ideas and beliefs on everything from economics to social welfare to America's place in the world. It has made me think about my beliefs in relation to the field to which I have devoted much of my life.

I believe that I have an obligation to become the very best I can be. That obligation is owed to all those who have given of themselves in my quest. I have a duty to light up my world and theirs with dazzling accomplishments which represent the very extreme of my capabilities. In doing so, I reward those from my past and inspire those in my present and future.

Mediocrity has a very strong pull, especially when fatigued or jaded. To remain committed to excellence and to help others do the same is a true test of character. It is deeds, not words, which define a person's worth.

Contributing to a win, and being welcomed into the dressing room by congratulations from your team-mates, makes that place, at that time, seem like the best place on earth.

Cricketers are people first, sportsmen second. Failing to see individuals as a complex set of personality traits, competing desires and unique backgrounds, is the biggest failure in management.

Cricket is a battle of will, talent and conviction. As an individual within a team, it falls upon each player to contribute to each other, in ways that matter. It is the responsibility of management to recognise and reward these efforts and to see through sham and bluster.

Each individual result on the cricket field is a culmination of an infinite number of preceding events. The recipe for success cannot be turned on and off, but needs to be lived every day of the year. The more often this is achieved, the greater the chance of success.

Every day should be cherished: our time to achieve all that we want is too limited to wish away.

Who knows what we can achieve, either over a period of time or in a particular moment? Be open minded to the possibility of doing well, of being extraordinary, of redefining who we are.

Statistics are reflections of the past: we are not slaves to the past, so ignore them.

There will be times when I will act in ways which I abhor, say things which I regret, and be a person I do not wish to be. So, when others do the same, practice humility not condemnation.

Tuesday 4 March

An extraordinary day. We were due to leave Uganda this morning and got as far as the end of the runway before we screeched to a halt, blew five of the tyres and were evacuated onto the tarmac. A warning light had apparently popped up just as the pilot was about to take off, requiring him to abort and hit the brakes as hard as possible. The manoeuvre left a few of the touring party a little weak in the knees.

Then the fun started. It turns out there are no spare tyres in Uganda, and the next flight isn't until next week. So we spent the morning and afternoon waiting around as this information slowly emerged, and worry grew that we would be stranded for another week. But, in this hour of need, up stepped Steve 'Superman' Salisbury. He battled with airport administration, grappled with incompetence and, through sheer bloody-mindedness and a refusal to take no for an answer, he managed to get us on an unscheduled flight to Nairobi and then onto a BA flight home. He emerged from his efforts looking slightly shaken and clearly drained, but buoyed by a sense of achievement at having done his duty for the MCC. What a man!

Chapter Three

Nottinghamshire

I don't really suffer from homesickness as such. I think it's because I don't identify myself with a particular place. Wherever I've been, whatever I've done, my enjoyment centres around the people who were there with me. As a result Nottingham evokes happy thoughts (so far!).

The changing room at Trent Bridge is long and thin with a supplementary room in the back to accommodate the burgeoning kit of the modern player. It is a slightly old-fashioned place in contrast to some of the newer, better proportioned but more sterile, changing rooms. Wooden benches form a spine down the middle. Lockers, handed down through the generations, line the walls. It seems as though the wood has absorbed something of the passing years, becoming a sweat-soaked, champagne-coated living witness to the cricket. There is a faint musty whiff when you walk in as though old people live there. During the summer there is always a waft of fresh toast which George and Eric, the dressing room attendants, serve up with tea and coffee to keep us happy. This is our home for the season, or a more appropriate term might be territory. For each man has staked an area, with cricket bags and shoes marking the boundaries. And there is a split. If you look left, you will see the bowlers: Franks, Shreck, Sidebottom, Pattinson, and Swann.

Paul Franks is methodical about his locker and surrounding area, demonstrating military-standard up-keeping. He has a prime spot: in the corner with his locker next to him and a great view of the ground. Paul made his county debut at 16 years of age and was the spearhead of the attack for several years. He has had to make the adjustment from strike bowler to one offering support, not an easy transition. Last year I went to his opening benefit event, a dinner at the East Midlands conference centre, a large venue holding around 500 people. It was filled to the rafters with local cricketers and supporters keen to show their fondness for a man who will move heaven and earth to play for his beloved Farnsfield CC on a Saturday.

Charlie Shreck is a lovely guy. That is a phrase that would make those batsmen who don't know him choke on their cornflakes. His on-field persona – grumpy, aggressive, contemptuous of the batsman's pathetic efforts – doesn't exactly win him many friends in the opposition. Off the field he can be found playing with his computer, a beast of a machine that he built himself and has more processing power than the Tardis, or something like that. His tall frame produces bounce and, with his wrist consistently behind the seam, he more often than not swings the ball. He is central to our bowling efforts and will need to play a pivotal role if we are to do well this year.

Between Charlie and Ryan is the Weather Window, the portal to the south-west. For years players would look out of it, often hoping for rain. When I joined last year, I unwittingly pitted myself against this cumulative meteorological experience.

I had looked at the radar provided by the Met Office and said that it was going to rain. "No chance, Wag." This was Mick, peering out of the window.

"Sorry, Mick, what was that?"

"No chance, nothing whatsoever in the weather window; it's not going to rain."

"But Mick, look at this, it's…," I said, trying to draw his attention to the computer screen.

"Twenty-seven years of experience I've had here. I don't care what your fancy computer says; I know I'm right."

Now remember I had just arrived at the club, and I was faced with a man completely convinced of the veracity of his contention. Nevertheless, in front of me, was a radar showing a huge band of rain about to hit Trent Bridge. So we had a bet, obviously. When the first raindrops splattered onto the glass, I probably overdid my celebrations. Slightly redder-faced than normal, Mick sloped off to his office to brood.

Ryan Sidebottom sits the other side of the window. His appearances are likely to be very limited this summer. Next to Ryan is newcomer Darren Pattinson. His route to the Trent Bridge dressing room is, I would guess, unique. Born in Grimsby he emigrated to Australia when he was six. Playing for a club side last year, he came along to nets on the recommendation of Dave Hussey. He bowled one ball: it was fast, straight and struck Gareth Clough solidly on the helmet. And that was all he could manage, his ankle producing too much pain to continue. But he had done enough to convince those watching that he was the genuine article. A three-year deal was duly put in the post to Melbourne.

At the end of the row is Graeme Swann, our dancing, singing, raconteur extraordinaire, off-spinning all-rounder. When Mick redesigned the team a few years ago, he wanted to recruit the best spinner in the country and so went after Graeme. His talent on the field is as multi-faceted as his antics off it.

The entrance to the back room is next to Graeme. In here Will Jefferson, Samit Patel and the younger guys change. The most striking feature of Will is obviously his height. He must have to say "six foot ten" at least a dozen times when he is out and about. He is very meticulous over his preparation, reads books like *The Magic of Thinking Big* and is very ambitious. He is also clever, speaks posh and is part of a very large family.

Samit has one way of thinking in almost every scenario: he is the best and will succeed. And that is true whether it is with the ball, the bat or any social situation. And this is one heck of a strength: utter faith in his ability. In fact, faith is completely the wrong word. For Samit his future success is a certainty, as inevitable as the sun rising in the morning. And he's talented, very talented. Wristy with the bat, surprisingly agile in the field and a much improved bowler.

To the right is the other half of the dressing room with the entrance to Mick's office at the end. Immediately next to me is the door to the physio's room. There is as much history in here as in the changing room, but it is the story of misfortune: splints, slings, crutches, bodily supports and a further multitude of medical knick-knacks fill the shelves and cupboards. It is in here that Craig Smith resides, banging out e-mails with the frequency of which a spammer would be proud. When not attached to his computer, Craig is generally regarded as one of the most accomplished physiotherapists in his field. He hails from Cape Town and not surprisingly returns there during the English winter. He is comfortably the worst footballer in the morning warm-ups, his tall, lean frame going into convulsions when in contact with the ball.

Back in the main dressing room I'm at the end of the bench, my space characterised by too much kit, not enough space. Next to me is Mark Ealham. Mark is crucial to the team as a go-to bowler in one-day cricket, the control man in four-day games and a match-changing batsman in all forms of the game. Mark is a real family man which helps him to retain a sense of balance when it comes to dealing with the variability of cricketing success. Whether he gets a duck or a century there isn't a great deal of difference in him, although he doesn't look forward to the grilling five-year-old George and three-year-old Tommy give him after a game.

Further along, in the corner, is Billy Shafayat. Slight of stature, Billy nevertheless has a gravitas about him, a maturity beyond his 23 years. He can bat, bowl, field, keep wicket, play football and he also runs an Indian take-away. He is always amiable company, rarely in a bad mood.

Next to Billy are the steps up to Mick's office.

As Director of Cricket, you might imagine Mick would have a rather plush office, a large desk, a plump comfortable chair. Instead, he has a bar stool, a piece of MDF fixed to the wall and a laptop. Throw in a couple of hooks on the walls and that is pretty much it. Mick is known as a lover of cricketing detail: along with Paul Franks, he will know, for example, the latest scores in a club game in north-west Pakistan, the most recent modes of dismissal of next week's batters, and will have read every post on the various cricketing forums.

Mick is a Nottinghamshire man: he played for the county from 1981 to 1991 and then took over from Clive Rice in the summer of 2002. I enjoy Mick's company: he listens, doesn't try to force respect and enjoys the general ribbing and banter that is central to any dressing room. There is a Jekyll and Hyde aspect to him, though; the moment a game of cricket starts, he can get somewhat tetchy and stressed. A rule of thumb I try to employ (but occasionally forget to my cost) is to avoid him during match time and tone down the banter. Mick isn't a coach in the traditional sense of someone who concerns himself with the technical side of a player's game. He does have the occasional thing to say about this, but most of his energy is engaged in the overall picture – the strategy for a game, team selection and the like, and the long-term make-up of the squad.

On this side of the dressing room, the prime spot belongs to Chris Read, the oft-reported best wicket-keeper in the country and captain of the team. He has his own bench, good shelving, and even his own mirror – facilities more than sufficient to garner plenty of envy. Chris is the ultimate professional – it would take an electron microscope to find any fat on him, he runs marathons for fun, and sets himself extremely high standards in everything he does. He takes on the captaincy at a point neutrals might say is not ideal: following Stephen Fleming, the stellar leader of men. But I think it says something about his standing within the team that there hasn't been a questioning word, and he seems to have fitted into his new role well. It will, I imagine, be a different managerial set-up this year. Last year, Mick worked very hard to provide an environment which Stephen could slot into and then run the show. I suspect that he will now take a more central role, working more in a partnership with Chris.

So that is the team. From the safety and comfort of the changing rooms, we walk out into the uncertainty of the game. And regardless of the result, it is here, to our familiar territories, that we return.

Last minute preparation

Oooh, those hands must be cold.
Mark Ealham prepares for another day.

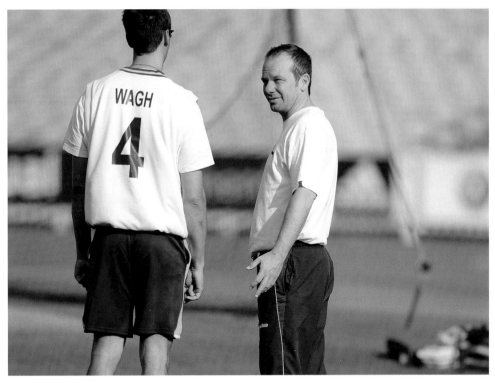

Affable Mick

Not ready yet

(back row) Kevin Paxton (fitness coach), Samit Patel, Rob Ferley, A
(middle row) Wayne Noon (assistant coach), Gareth Clough, Mark Wagh, Darren Pa
(front row) Brian Hewes (scorer), Stuart Broad, Ryan Sidebottom, Adam Voges, Mick N

s, Luke Fletcher, Mark Footitt, Bilal Shafayat, Craig Smith (physio)
Will Jefferson, Charlie Shreck, AJ Harris, Matt Wood, Paul Johnson (batting coach)
oach), Chris Read, Mark Ealham, Paul Franks, Graeme Swann, Roger Marshall (scorer)

Darren Pattinson, the find of the summer

The airplane lands. Samit celebrates another wicket.

Little and Large: Billy Shafayat (5'7") and Will Jefferson (6'10")

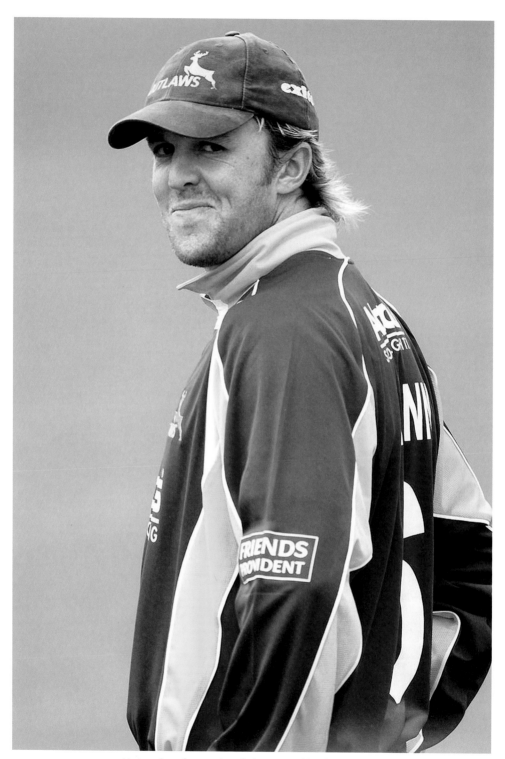

Not only a fantastic wit but good looks as well.
Graeme Swann spots the photographer.

Chapter Four

March

Friday 7 March
Trent Bridge

I have just come back from a much needed massage. The first three days of pre-season have been fairly tough with our new fitness coach, Kevin Paxton, wanting to put down a marker. He is a fairly austere individual – slightly unsure, I think, of what to make of us. We are certainly a varied bunch, ranging from the gnarled old veteran Ealham to the youths dipping their toes into their first pre-season.

Watching these youngsters has made me reflect on how I would have come across to my Warwickshire team mates when I first started. I would have been full of the self-importance that comes from three years at university where we were taught that debate was good and that our opinions counted. An excellent grounding for academia, but less advantageous in an environment where junior pros had only recently been admitted into the main dressing room. I found the transition from a relatively egalitarian society to a keenly hierarchical one difficult, and I don't think I handled it in the best way. I remember having a strong argument with Neil Smith in front of the whole team, tenaciously fighting my corner. Over what, I have no idea. I probably came across as obnoxious and arrogant. It was ended when Ashley Giles stood up and said something along the lines of because I was a junior I was wrong and should shut up. It cut to the very heart of what I believed and left me fairly devastated. I should have been less assertive in defending my worthiness as an individual; I wish I had realised that I could have acquiesced publicly without permanently giving up the right to matter. I should also have had more appreciation of the hard work and talent required to remain a professional sportsman for several years and proffered respect on the basis of time served. In my defence, the culture within dressing rooms was evolving: the old days of senior and junior were being replaced by a much flatter structure. When I started, my elders were the last generation to have had to bow and scrape to their seniors, and I think they partly felt it should be time for them to benefit.

I am really enjoying being back, though. It gives me a sense of purpose, brings the season closer, validates me if you like. I love running at that level just beyond comfortable but not into the painful category. I love practising skills that I can put to use in a few weeks. Generally everyone feels pretty good about their own game in pre-season, that's what it's designed to do. But I'm really excited by the challenge this year, fascinated to see what I can achieve.

Incidentally, I mentioned to Mick and Chris my slight concern regarding our expectation levels for the coming season. They both took my comments well.

Monday 10 March

A classic pre-season day: cricket skills in the morning and fitness in the afternoon. The morning was spent at Loughborough in the ECB cricket facility. I had an 'open' net in which three bowlers bowled at me with the nets pulled back, in an attempt to mimic match conditions. It works to a degree, and it was a good test on the bouncy indoor surface. I felt as though I was prodding at the ball, and my feet weren't working as well as I would have hoped. Nevertheless, I was waiting for the ball reasonably well most of the time. This was despite the presence of my net nemesis, Mark Footitt, a left-arm fast bowler whom I am most grateful plays for us. If I survive a ball in the nets from him, it comes as a huge surprise to me. He must rub his hands with glee when he sees me on the roster when he is bowling!

When I first get to the wicket, sometimes anxiety about a particular delivery makes me move too early in an attempt to cover that ball, and I have to remind myself to trust my ability to react in time and play the correct shot. If everything seems to be happening too quickly, this is the first thing I come back to – slow down, stay still and wait for the ball.

Fitness was a biathlon: 20 minutes both on the bike and the running machine. It was a decent workout, and I did some weights after the session. I feel strength is important to my game as well as my general health and fitness. It seems that the stronger I am, the better I feel, and the better I play. Both Dad and his dad were weight lifters and I seem to have inherited the same enthusiasm (if not the physique!). Kevin seems to be loosening up a little and is proving to be good company. It's vital that the fitness coach has a very good relationship with the players, so the signs are promising.

This evening I had a meal with Ealham, Read, Ferley and Franks. We chatted about England, the ICL, the training we've been doing and food.

Food is an emotive subject for cricketers: if you want to woo a cricketer, food is your greatest ally. When the fixture list is published, eager eyes scan the away grounds, not for the potential wicket, the practice facilities or anything so frivolous – the only concern is the culinary offering. I've lost count of the number of times I've discussed the merits of various venues; compiled top fives (Lord's, Northampton, Edgbaston, Leicester and Canterbury); cogitated, deliberated and digested. If you browse through a *Cricketers Who's Who*, you'll see food appearing a startling number of times in interests and opinions on cricket.

When I say food, I really mean desserts. Nick Knight's wife, Trudie, used to make him a dessert for every century he scored (and he scored a lot of them, she must have been forever baking!). The old-fashioned staples of spotted dick, bread and butter pudding or (my personal favourite) banoffee pie can lift the spirits of an entire team far better than any Churchillian words from the captain.

Wednesday 12 March

We are in the departure hall at Heathrow airport, on the way to Pretoria for two weeks' fitness and cricket. These trips are de rigueur for most teams although the destinations vary depending on the club finances. Last year we were in Portugal so clearly things are looking up.

I've been walking around the shops. My love for all things gadgety took me to Dixons, trying to find something that will justify me spending some money.

Now, sipping coffee, I can see Mark Ealham and Chris Read peering into an Audi R8, the prize in a lottery draw. These two petrolheads are no doubt discussing the torque-to-BHP ratio or something. Further afield, Paul Franks and Will Jefferson are browsing through the clothes in Hugo Boss, whilst the youngsters, Hales, Fletcher and Carter, look like they are buying enough DVDs to keep them going for a few months. Over there in the corner I think I can see Mick and assistant coach Wayne Noon sipping a beer in a quiet corner of the pub. And here comes Kevin Paxton, walking faster than most people run. He's got headphones the size of laundry baskets attached to his ears so is oblivious to me calling him.

And there is the call to board, so I've got ten hours of moderate discomfort to look forward to (better let Kevin know!).

Friday 14 March

Pretoria

We are staying in rudimentary digs at the High Performance Centre in the University campus. There was some grumbling when we arrived and were allocated to our respective accommodation. Half the squad is in the recently built main building which boasts swanky rooms with wireless internet and satellite TV. The rest of us are in a less salubrious, concrete prison block with mildew and rising damp the only features to mention.

The cricket facilities though are excellent. Fitness, fielding and netting are the order of the day so far with five days of games coming up. Last night, an enormous electrical storm came through; the volume of rain was something else. Yet, somehow, the net surfaces and outfield seem to have coped easily. The forecast for the next few days, however, is worryingly more of the same.

During pre-season we become sheep-like, herded from one venue or activity to the next. It's a time to keep your head down, stay focused on the bigger picture. I really enjoy fitness work and all the practice drills associated with this time of year, but I prefer working under my own steam. I realise, of course, it's impossible to accommodate each person's whims and foibles, so I shall have to heed my own advice and keep my head down.

Sunday 16 March

It's raining. Heavily. A morning gym session and now we are assessing our leisure options for the afternoon. Staying in the complex is definitely not popular but transport is an issue. My money is on a cinema trip at some point. So some time for reflection.

I started playing cricket at quite a young age when my uncle took me down to the compound of his apartment in Mumbai to play cricket with the other boys. I have very hazy memories of the time, but uncle assures me I was OK!

It was a chance conversation that took me to Warwickshire. My mum was waiting to pick me up outside Harborne Junior School when she started chatting to a fellow mum. She mentioned how easily I got bored, and in reply the other mum said that her son went to Edgbaston and played cricket. So I was whisked down to the county ground and into the hands of Alan Townsend. Alan was a superb coach whose kind-heartedness and good humour ensured a loyal following to his Sunday morning sessions. I used to get there early in the hope that, once everyone had had a bat, I might get a second innings at the end.

My childhood from that point and subsequently my adolescence was cricket heavy, with weekends and school holidays filled with practice or matches. Because I showed some promise, I played in age groups above my own. This was undoubtedly good for my cricket, but it affected my social development in that I rarely interacted with my peers outside school time. We are all products of our upbringing to some degree and, in order to fit in with older people, I didn't want to appear young and immature. This has at times made me feel inhibited, unable truly to let go, but equally I loved playing in these teams as the young 'star' and through these years I developed ambition and determination. In retrospect, I think I was perhaps too ambitious, always looking forward, extrapolating today's form into the distant future, rather than enjoying the day.

I went on to King Edward's School, Birmingham (no one more surprised than me when I passed the entrance exam). It was here that comparisons with Anurag Singh started. Anurag went on to play for Warwickshire, Worcestershire and Nottinghamshire without really establishing himself. Anurag was a year older, but we played in the same teams at school and at Warwickshire. He was a fantastically talented batsman, searingly intelligent and very driven. At times it felt as though I was in direct competition with him; match results didn't matter as long as I scored more runs. I think the greatest effect his presence had on me was that it made me want to differentiate myself from him. So whilst he was confident, cocky even, I tended towards introversion; as he was almost obsessed with his game, I tried to affect a laid-back air; anything to draw a line between us. It was also another aspect of the competition between us: if he rubbed people up the wrong way with his brashness, I could garner popularity by being self-deprecating. I'm not sure how much was calculated and how much was just natural, but I'm fairly ashamed to admit most of it. Rivalry is part of growing up. Even so, I wish I had dealt with it better.

Sunday 23 March

The tour is going well. Everyone is working well in the gym, and the outdoor practice is of a high standard. There is a slightly different team dynamic from last year, with a higher proportion of younger guys in this group. It's not quite a first-team squad as a few key members are missing (Swann, Shreck and Voges).

I'm reading Gabriel Garcia Marquez's *One Hundred Years of Solitude*. It's enjoyable, but I can't help feeling I'm missing something as various luminaries have described it as the best novel of the last 50 years/ever. Mark Ealham is enjoying Jeremy Clarkson's *And Another Thing*. Every few minutes he chuckles and hands me the book, pointing out the funny line. It seems as though Clarkson is validating the beliefs of our slightly un-PC, slightly right-wing stalwart.

Mark is a highly skilled cricketer, and his performances on the pitch have earned him the respect and affection of players and supporters alike. I change next to him and love his irreverent, grumpy-old-man humour. One of his nicknames is 'Sapper', putatively because he saps the energy of the group with his down-trodden, negative take on life. Nothing could be further from the truth in my opinion. He verbalises what everyone is feeling, and by doing so with a cheeky smile often clears the air or turns a sore point into a funny moment. He knows that there are times when he has to be careful, where his style might not be appropriate, and he admits that he occasionally gets it wrong. But that is the case for everyone, as I know only too well. There are very few times in our lives when we feel totally able to relax, to be who we are without fear of upsetting someone; the rest of the time requires some self-censorship. Mark also has an excellent brain, seeing the long view when everyone else is caught up in the heat of the moment. With the absence of Fleming this year, we are going to need his cool head and wealth of experience.

Tuesday 25 March

We won our final one-day game of the tour today. Samit Patel and Will Jefferson knocked off the runs with aplomb. My room-mate, Luke Fletcher, has impressed with Angus Fraser-like seamers. He is 18 years old, enjoys bowling and is prepared to put in the hard yards; it looks like he has a decent future in the game. Should he fail at the game, I'm fairly sure a career in comedy would be an option. He has the ability to make people laugh purely by being himself. He is ingenuous, utterly sincere and everything he says or does is completely uncontrived. A very funny man indeed.

He is part of the youthful triumvirate we have on this trip, the other two being Alex Hales, a batter from London, and Andy Carter, a fast bowler from Lincolnshire. This is their first pre-season trip and is clearly a steep learning curve for them all, not just from the cricket point of view but also team dynamics. They are also being 'beasted' by Kevin in the gym, a sight which brings a few chuckles from the rest of us.

My form with the bat has been modest: a couple of 20s in my two innings. It's easy to hide behind the fact that these games have been low key, and I will need to step up my level of intensity soon. Technically my game seems reasonably solid; I just need to swing well and retain positive expectations.

I have enjoyed the company of Wayne Noon this trip. Wayne used to keep wicket for Notts and is primarily in charge of the second team. When I first arrived on the staff last year, I think Wayne was a little unsure of what to make of me. This seems to be a too-common occurrence, but at least he has remained open-minded and I think we get on well now. He has a passion to see people do well, and he thrives on the day-to-day personal contact with his players. On tour, he often leaves his door open, encouraging others to pop in and have a chat. His partnership with Mick is important because they see different cricket during the summer so Mick needs to trust Wayne's judgment. He was the one who spotted Luke and is justifiably pleased that he is showing the potential he would have promoted to Mick. He only takes on a few cricketers each year, a stance I think is correct. A scattergun approach to signing young players is simply a way for a coach to cover his back, with credit being claimed if one of the many actually succeeds, whilst conveniently forgetting the other dozen or so cricketers who have fallen by the wayside. It's also not particularly fair on the cricketers themselves, as there aren't enough games or practice time to invest in each of them.

Monday 31 March
Trent Bridge

Back at TB and a superb day's practice: uninterrupted sunshine allowed us to have outdoor nets and fielding practice morning and afternoon. The PCA (Professional Cricketers' Association) spoke to us, as they do each year, addressing the most pressing areas which affect us as players. Obviously the IPL/ICL situation took up much of the meeting, but the issue of 12-month contracts and the domestic structure also cropped up. There seems to be an almost febrile atmosphere within the administration of the game at the moment, with projection and extrapolation fuelling relatively radical suggestions as to the best way forward. What worries me slightly is that the IPL will be used as a cover to introduce ideas long held by some but which have previously, in less threatening times, failed to gain support. I hope that good judgment remains at the forefront in any decision-making process and doesn't get swept to the sidelines by apocryphal claims about the impact of IPL. It's worth bearing in mind that, as yet, it is a totally untested product in India.

Chapter Five

County cricket

If nothing else, the modern professional cricketer has to be able to adapt to the various forms of the game. With the possibility of a game lasting just five overs or being a four-day marathon, county cricket tests the full extent of a cricketer's abilities.

It can be difficult to switch mindsets when going from a Championship game to a one-dayer. A simple example is the ball just outside off stump. In a four-day game, this should probably be left alone, as playing at it risks the ball going to the slips. But this is exactly the desired outcome in a one-day game, free as that area usually is of predatory fielders. So, in one form of the game, the correct instinctive reaction is to leave, and in the other to play.

When you remember that an instinctive reaction is, by definition, out of conscious control, and each one is built on the basis of thousands upon thousands of balls of practice, just how the brain switches from one to the other is boggling.

It's not a perfect mechanism however, as techniques from one form of the game can sometimes leak into the others. This isn't always a bad thing. The best shot I've played in my career was a hit over the bowler's head for six from a good-length, swinging ball. Hampshire's Sean Ervine was the bowler down at the Rose Bowl, and I don't know who was more shocked, him or me. Disappointingly this is the only time I've achieved such a feat, despite numerous failed attempts to emulate it.

What helps the transition from long to short form is that much of what is done in one-day cricket is premeditated. A batsman will be thinking, as the bowler runs up, "If the ball is in this area, I'll hit it over there." If you take these calculated shots out of the equation, the techniques between the forms are not that different. The fundamentals are very similar, but there is a different reward system, favouring a higher risk strategy in the one-day game.

This is true for bowlers as well. Wickets are obviously important, but the emphasis is primarily on run restriction. So a spinner may bowl differently in one-day cricket, though he must not become predictable as batsmen will pounce on that. He must remain one step ahead of the batsmen, making spin bowling in one-day cricket as much a test of mind-reading as it is of the bowling action.

An important effect of multiple formats of the game is that it begets an increasing skill set. There are so many different scenarios during a season, in terms of score, fielding position and risk required, that a successful county cricketer needs to have a wide repertoire of available responses.

One area that is very different and requires, indeed demands, a different approach, is the energy levels between the formats. The shorter the format, the more intense the action and the more physically arduous it is. After a tough four-day game, it can be a very difficult transition to make! And equally, after the high of a one-day victory with its high-energy cricket, it can be difficult to adjust to the lower-key, slow-burning intensity of a four-day game. This can be exacerbated by playing in front of a full house one day and a smattering of spectators the next.

Personally I love the changing formats. It refreshes tired minds and brings colour, in every way, to a season.

So what does it take to be triumphant in this era? Looking back over the time I've been playing, Surrey and Sussex have been the most successful four-day teams winning the Championship three times each, whilst Yorkshire, Warwickshire and Nottinghamshire have all won once.

In six out of nine years, a champion spinner has been the driving force, first Saqlain Mushtaq and then Mushtaq Ahmed. Yorkshire and Nottinghamshire had strong seam attacks, and in 2004 Warwickshire batted the opposition into submission.

Most of English domestic one-day cricket is played on used wickets, making the role of the spinner as important as in the Championship. Coaches have long realised that the signing of a 'magic' spinner could be the single most important piece of the winning jigsaw. Having a spin bowler toiling away at one end allows the other bowlers to remain fresh. So not only are you battling to survive at one end, there's no let up at the other! Spinners also tend to get injured less often than fast bowlers and can be effective irrespective of the state of the ball.

Possibly the most magic of all the spinners, Muttiah Muralitharan, has had only limited exposure to the county circuit, but he almost single-handedly won every game he played in, either for Lancashire or for Kent. Mushtaq Ahmed turned a very good Sussex team into trophy-machine county. And in star-studded Surrey the biggest star was off-spinning, top-spinning Saqlain Mushtaq.

When these guys first came onto the circuit, there was a great deal of consternation. I remember a game at Edgbaston against Surrey in 1999. Saqlain was taking wickets for fun that year, and we had kindly prepared a spinning surface for him. All the batters before the game were trying to tap into Nick Knight's experience of having faced him on tour, trying to work out how to 'pick' him.

I had already been dismissed when he came on and was watching from the committee room in the pavilion where all the players gathered. I was with Dougie Brown, the next man in. "Easy – off-spinner ... toppie ...

toppie," he called as Saqlain bowled his over. Dougie had this earnestness about everything he said, eyes on beanstalks, utterly innocent, impossible not to believe he was completely committed to what he was saying. "Offie … top spinner …" This went on until a wicket fell. Doug, looking suitably confident, scooped up his helmet, bat and gloves and walked out the door accompanied by the usual calls of "good luck," "go well," etc.

Doug had one of the best defences against spin, pushing his bat out well in advance of his front pad, ensuring there was no chance of a bat-pad chance. So, with relative ease, Dougie negotiated the first ball he faced with a perfect forward block. But then that much-advertised ability to read Saqlain must have gone slightly awry as, second ball, he advanced down the track and tried to whip the ball over mid-wicket. Unfortunately it was the 'toppie', and the ball just looped to extra cover.

I'm not quite sure who let out the first yelping laugh, unable to contain it any longer, but I can say that by the time Dougie had reached the gate, shaking his head in disbelief, the committee room was full of utterly inappropriate side-splitting laughter and teary eyes.

Since those times I think county batters are better prepared, having had some experience of playing this type of bowling. That's not to say a quality spinner can't be very successful, but simply that it won't be as easy.

In the same way that there have only been a handful of special spinners, there have only been a few exceptional captains. Captaincy is a very difficult job at any level. Making the tactical and strategic decisions, being the main motivator and counsellor, as well as maintaining their own form, make it an exceptionally challenging role.

It's appropriate that I mention Stephen Fleming first as he was one of the reasons I came to Nottingham. He had a tremendous presence, his deep sonorous voice combined with his large imposing frame to convey a sense of assurance; it seemed natural to have confidence in whatever he was saying or doing. He was a very laid-back captain, not looking to be involved in everything that was going on. But there was an element of awkwardness in him in some ways as well. At times, it was as if a child was peeping out from behind this commanding man. For the most part, however, he was the central stanchion around which we could gather. He was like a parent offering a secure environment for us children to play without worry; we would just do our thing, and he would make sure everything would work out well.

He was central to Nottinghamshire winning the Championship in 2005. He allowed all the elements Mick had assembled to come together and form a winning combination. And it shouldn't be forgotten, overshadowed as it sometimes was by his captaincy, Stephen was a fantastic batsman.

For what he had clearly helped to create at Sussex, Chris Adams is someone for whom I have a great deal of respect. There's no doubt that having Mushtaq to bowl almost continuously from one end made his job as captain much easier. But what has impressed me from outside is the environment within the team: there is a real togetherness, a clear understanding of roles and, most importantly, a great deal of success.

The final two exceptional captains can be grouped together because they share many qualities. Shane Warne and Adam Hollioake were ultra-charismatic leaders in the truest sense. In whatever sphere these two would have chosen, I bet that they would have risen to lead. They commanded attention, not through japes or antics but purely through their presence.

They often brought themselves into the game when it was in the balance, intent on winning the game for their team. I don't think Warne had quite the mesmeric effect in the county game as he did in the international arena (perhaps needing that extra incentive to bring out the best in him) but they both had an uncanny knack of taking wickets or scoring runs just at the right time. I think it's fair to say that, without these two at the helm, regardless of their personal performance with bat and ball, Surrey wouldn't have been as successful as they were and Hampshire wouldn't have won so many games.

I commentated on a Friends Provident semi-final last year between Hampshire and Warwickshire at the Rose Bowl. Warwickshire had taken the surprising decision not to play Ian Bell, deciding Ian Westwood would be a better bet. Hampshire batted first and scored 206 for seven, an average score at best.

In contrast to Warwickshire's rather formulaic approach to the field settings and bowling changes, Warne was dynamic with a novel plan seemingly for every batsman. It was beguiling to watch and must have been impossible to play against, as it appeared Warne was one step ahead for the whole innings.

The only point during which it looked as if Warwickshire might mount a challenge was when Kumar Sangakkara was batting with Jim Troughton. They struck the ball cleanly and seemed to have a firm grip on the game. It was a crucial juncture, and Warne brought himself on. Out of the blue he convinced Troughton to try to hit him over long on, taking on the longest boundary. The ball just carried to the man who was perfectly placed. It was the turning point in the game, heralding the collapse. Hampshire won by 40 runs.

It is much harder to pick common factors when it comes to success in one-day cricket, and especially Twenty20. It seems as though each winning team comes up with its own formula.

There is, however, one vitally important ingredient – spin, again! Through the middle overs in any format of the one-day game, spin tends to dominate. With the field out, low-risk cricket tends to predominate and spinners can squeeze the life out of an innings. Taking the pace off the ball requires courage but can be incredibly successful (remember Jeremy Snape's 'moon ball'?).

The other area that teams work very hard on is 'death' bowling, those last few overs of an innings where bowlers try to bowl yorkers, slower balls and the occasional bouncer whilst the batsmen try anything and everything to get the ball over the ropes. These overs often decide a game, and it takes a certain type of bowler to succeed in these conditions. A cool head, a reliable yorker and a bit of luck are the determinants of success.

But it wouldn't surprise me if in the next twelve months other methods have proved successful, such is the speed of evolution in the short game. Perhaps raw pace will become the special ingredient or batsmen/ techniques will be recruited from major league baseball?

Being a county cricketer is a helter-skelter profession, with the requirements shifting day to day. The intensity of the game is the highest it has ever been and set to increase as greater monies come in. In the same week, a day can start and end before you realise and at other times Old Father seems to meander, almost crawl, on his way.

Chapter Six

Early weeks

Tuesday 15 April

Canterbury

I see that there has been a bit of a gap since my last entry. I haven't felt that there has been much to write about. Pre-season preparation rolled on, with nets, fitness and practice matches. After a while, I found it all a bit meaningless. I have felt 'ready' for a while. But today I have a spring in my step, and practice down here in Kent on the eve of the season, bathed in wonderful sunshine, has brought everything back into sharp focus. I need it to matter: for good shots to count, efforts in the field to carry weight. Mick spoke excellently this afternoon, not so much about the mechanics of four-day cricket (essentially: batters watch the ball and react, aim to get 400 on the board, bowlers hit top of off stump), but about the fact that we were a group taking Nottingham into a new era, with each of us committed to several years at the club. He also mentioned how we were favourites for relegation. This can be a dangerous tactic, but I came away with a sense that we were in it together, hoping that we will all pitch in to make this year a success.

In the chat about Kent, Mark, as the local, gave us the run down on their bowlers. "Robbie Joseph, well he's put on a yard, bowls close to 85 mph, with a decent bouncer. Swings it, always swings it, and it's often late swing."

The batsmen all look round; a modicum of fleeting concern can be sensed.

"Martin Saggers, rarely bowls a bad ball, swings it both ways. He's pretty nippy with a great surprise bouncer. And he also has the ability to go wide of the crease, pitch it on the straight and move it away to the slips."

This wasn't what Mick and Chris had anticipated. It certainly wasn't what the batters wanted to hear. The longer Mark spoke, the further our chances rescinded. He continued in a similar vein. When he finished, silence.

"So, Eals," I eventually said. "What you're saying is … good luck!"

Luke Fletcher, my room-mate in Pretoria, has made it into the final twelve. It's a great effort from someone who was playing club cricket last year. He has impressed with almost every spell and without question is more than capable of playing and doing well tomorrow.

Unlike Mark I'm not intending to mention the opposition too much in this diary, as I feel I shall end up repeating myself. To generalise: all teams will have several quality batters, a number of very decent bowlers and one or two star performers. Primarily sport is about challenge, both macro and micro, and one's reaction is the fun part. I know that I will feel uncertain, fearful, invincible, confident, content, depressed, elated, despondent and every other flavour of the smorgasbord of emotion over the coming months. That much I take for granted: what I don't know, is how I will react.

Wednesday 16 April

Canterbury, County Championship – Day One
Kent 162 all out (Pattinson 5-22, Shreck, 4-65)
Nottinghamshire 121 for three (Wagh 52*)

The season has started! Canterbury has been one of the most picturesque grounds; the slightly ramshackle nature of the stands, combined with the lime tree, gave it an attractive quaintness. Today, however, it just looked tired. It was freezing cold, the old tree has been replaced with a sapling and the stands were all but empty.

Nonetheless we were all fired up this morning. Darren Pattinson bowled superbly to take five wickets on debut and, with Charlie Shreck bagging four, formed a potent new-ball partnership. It was an impressive bowling display and bodes well for the summer.

In our reply, I played well in testing, swinging conditions. The most pleasing aspect was that it gave me a sense that I am capable of getting runs in this division: talk of a gulf in standards between the divisions was causing some angst. Doubt is a perpetual voice in my career, sometimes whispering, other times vociferously clamouring for attention. I feel better prepared to answer it now, and I enjoy the challenge.

We are in an excellent position, something to calm the nerves, and it gives us something to work on for the rest of the game. Early season points can be vital so let's hope we can capitalise tomorrow.

Thursday 17 April

Canterbury, County Championship – Day Two
Kent 162 and 14 for no wicket
Nottinghamshire 434 for nine dec (Ealham 130*, Patel 54, Franks 52, Wagh 52)

Of course it is disappointing to get out first over today; it's incredibly frustrating to be sitting here in the pavilion. I started the day with real hope of scoring a lot of runs; I'd prepared well last night, slept reasonably (I never sleep that soundly when not out over night), and hit them well in warm-up. And the result of all that? Bowled second ball!

This game will almost definitely have a result. As usual at this time of the year the weather could play a deciding factor, and today there is a bracing easterly taking temperatures down to about 5°C.

Mark Ealham has scored a brilliant hundred against his old chums. He was belligerent, bullying and unstoppable, bringing up the century with a six. He has this ability to turn games. Indeed, situations that are in the balance bring out the best in him.

A lighter moment: Luke Fletcher, trying to close the patio door to the changing door, merely succeeds in pushing it off its hinges and shattering the glass. Luke and Mick spend the rest of the day picking up glass. Luke's face a picture.

Later

I've spoken to Jamil and have started to wonder whether I should look to dominate more, not in a physically aggressive way but by weight of runs. Raise my level of expectation. Not be happy with simply proving to myself that I can cope. This sounds childishly simple, but a slight change in emphasis can have huge reverberations in the rest of your game. And that realisation that I need to prove to myself that I can cope is a real eye-opener. I'll have to think about that today and see what comes out.

Friday 18 April

Canterbury, County Championship – Day Three
Kent 162 and 293 all out
Nottinghamshire 434 for nine declared

Frustratingly we are off the field for bad light. So far we have played excellent cricket. Today we have bowled with perseverance and heart. Mark's innings has completely redefined this match: what I thought would be a close nail-biter now sees us with a huge first innings lead and firmly in the box seats. With a poor weather forecast tomorrow, we need to get back out tonight if possible. Azhar Mahmood has played with aggressive intent and is 101 not out. It's a timely reminder that something worthwhile can be achieved on a day which is as far from a summer's day as it is possible to be. The temperature, with wind chill, is about 3 or 4°C; a grey, dour sky has offered little in the way of inspiration. Our Antipodean team members were scrambling for thermal layers and woolly hats this morning, and a key requirement for everyone whilst on the field has been to maintain a reasonable core body temperature – not an easy feat.

Saturday 19 April

Canterbury, County Championship – Day Four
Kent 162 and 293 all out
Nottinghamshire 434 for nine declared and 24 for no wicket
Nottinghamshire won by ten wickets

Sunday 20 April

Edgbaston, Friends Provident Trophy versus Warwickshire
Rained off

Monday 21 April

Nottingham

We had a recovery session this morning at the local gym. Our usual routine is that after a game we have a 30-minute stretch in the pool. I did a few lengths afterwards in the outdoor pool. I really enjoy outdoor swimming; the contrast between warm water and cool air invigorates, and I end up feeling refreshed but also worked.

We managed to get out on Friday and then for 20 minutes on Saturday to complete a very satisfying victory. I am excited by the team we have at the moment, especially as Sidebottom and Broad are going to join us for the next two championship games. I guess when they leave us for the international arena, along with Graeme Swann, we might be a little bare in the bowling department should injuries infiltrate the fold. We also need to make sure that our top five batters score heavily, allowing the middle to lower order to turn a good score into an excellent one.

I've had a few text messages from Dave Hussey. He seems to be enjoying the IPL, but he says the pressure is huge. I watched a little of one of the games last night and it's clear that, with so much money at stake, usually calm people are living every ball, fear and elation skipping across their faces like cloud shadows on a windy day. It's captivating stuff, and it appears to be well received.

I have this week off. The guys are playing Oxford University, but Mick has decided a week of gym and nets will be more beneficial. Actually he said, "I'm never playing you in a non-competitive game again, you're a waste of space in those games," something which brought a chuckle from the boys. I couldn't disagree.

I think I might pop down to see how they are getting on, perhaps on Wednesday. I also noted that a chap called Morse was opening the bowling for Oxford. If I were coach, I would scour the place for a Lewis.

Wednesday 23 April

Oxford

Picturesque doesn't even get close. The sun has brought out the very best of the Parks, reminding me of some very happy memories of my time here.

When I was elected captain of Oxford for the '97 season, I immediately asked Roger Newman to come on board. For a large proportion of my development Roger has been part-mentor/part-coach. It is wrong to lay blame or credit at one person's door as so many people have had an effect on my progress, forwards and backwards. Sometimes it only takes a suggestion, a nuance on a situation at just the right time that can turn things around. However, if only for his doggedness in sticking by me over the years, Roger deserves special mention. He was the first-team coach at King Edward's and drafted me into the team when I was 13. This was somewhat revolutionary as playing cricketers out of their age group was only just coming in, and then only a year or two up. But convention has always been a red rag waiting to be shredded by the Newman horns, and this selection decision alone made my time in school cricket worthwhile. I remember Roger's enthusiasm most of all. It was as though we kids had to calm *him* down on match days, as he chuffed his way through a packet of B&H to take the edge off his nerves. As the years passed, I realised he also had great intuition about my game, making suggestions which, although sometimes it would take weeks or even months for me to accept, were more often than not excellent.

Roger proposed getting Andy Flower involved. I had played club cricket with Andy at West Bromwich Dartmouth and, at that stage in mid-1996, his international career was just about to take off. It proved to be an excellent appointment as they formed a fantastic partnership – very different people but each respectful of the other's talents. Andy was all steel, ferociously determined, with an extensive and detailed knowledge of the game. Roger was loquacious, creative and possessed an innate ability to motivate and encourage second to none. Between the two of them, they produced an environment in which each of us was stimulated to become the best cricketers we could be.

I think one of the reasons I loved that season so much was that I was in control. As captain, along with Roger and Andy, I was charged with taking this group of people and making them into a team. Nobody expected much at all, but that level of expectation didn't sit well with me or with Roger and Andy. For many of the guys, it would be their only first-class season, their one chance to bowl at the likes of Graeme Hick or Nick Knight and face Ashley Giles or Robert Croft, so they wanted memories of which to be proud. And nobody enjoys losing, whether it's expected or not. Beating

Glamorgan that summer is one of my most treasured memories. In the surreal moments after the game in the dressing room, it was almost as if we needed assurance that we really had won.

Nowadays, of course, there isn't really such a thing as Oxford University CC, instead it is a Centre of Excellence with students from the former polytechnic Oxford Brookes eligible to play. In fact, the team is primarily sourced from Brookes, a state of affairs which saddens me slightly. There is always I suppose a certain nostalgia when revisiting places which echo with long-past laughter, and a natural desire to replicate those circumstances which produced such happy times. Perhaps it is possible to argue that the current set-up is more beneficial, efficient, or whatever else the administrators may wish to call it, but I can't help feeling something special has been lost.

Saturday 26 April
Dublin

It's the start of the Friends Provident 50-over competition for us tomorrow. We have our strongest possible team available as Sidebottom and Broad have come across. In fact we seem to have brought virtually everyone, along with their spouses and offspring. It has the air of a jaunt rather than a job. I enjoy the company of all the wives and girlfriends, indeed they add tremendously to proceedings but, because the air tickets were booked several months ago and guesses had to be taken as to who would be in the squad, we have ended up with a large cumbersome group.

This sounds very bah-humbug now that I've re-read it, and I guess if I had an 'other half' then I would be adding to the 'cumbersome group'. Preparation is also very much an individual thing, and each must do what is best for them. I'm a little tired but looking forward to the game tomorrow. The weather forecast has improved, and we should get a game in.

Off to the bar to try a proper pint of Guinness …

Sunday 27 April
Dublin, Friends Provident Trophy
Nottinghamshire 217 for nine (50 overs, Voges 60, Read 45, Wagh 0)
Ireland 161 all out (45.3 overs, Ealham 4-39)
Nottinghamshire won by 56 runs

A comfortable victory, despite being 19 for three. Adam Voges played well for 60 on a turgid, slow club wicket. I failed to score, deciding to leave one which nipped back a little and thudded into off stump. These games are always a potential banana skin, so it's pleasing to get through.

Graeme Swann contributed in all departments. It's noticeable how both he and Ryan Sidebottom have improved since they have played for England. Graeme's control is superb, and he seems more composed with the bat whilst Ryan swings the ball later and at greater pace. I guess international cricket stimulates and catalyses development and, of course, leaves the players brimming with confidence when they return to the county ranks.

Monday 28 April

Dublin Airport

I feel a little flat today. My mood is often directly correlated to runs scored. It sounds selfish, but it's true. Obviously when we win it mitigates the disappointment (and a loss exaggerates); nevertheless, the underlying feeling remains. It centres around a desire to contribute. It also touches on the issue of success and failure.

Success and failure are two constant companions. In theory, I suppose, it should be a continuum: success at one end, failure at the other, each outcome fitting in somewhere on the scale with its unique mixture of some success, some failure. So scoring 60 should feel more successful than, say, 50. Emotionally, however, I think it's more binary: an event feels either a success or a failure. Of course there are variations in intensity around these two poles (a 150 feels in a different realm to a 60) but it is hard to get away from the rudimentary emotional appraisal.

The opiate of success is what keeps me coming back for more. There is nothing better than sitting in a changing room after you've won the game, having personally contributed to that win. It gives meaning to all the training, the mental and physical effort, it's the pay-off for risking failure. There aren't too many jobs where one's prowess is broadcast to the public on a daily basis. It can be fantastic; it can be hell.

But there are some things that are lost to everyone but yourself. If I'm batting well, time can seem to slow down after the ball is released. The sense of my body moving in synchronicity with the approaching ball, the bat coming through in almost slow motion and then that moment of agonising anticipation just on contact when it seems I'm holding my breath, waiting, and then the joy, the beautiful feedback through the bat, hands, and arms, that I've timed the ball perfectly – success!

It could be argued that one's ability to cope with failure is a crucial determinant in the long-term success of a career, because one is likely to experience it more often: even the great Sir Donald Bradman only hit a century every three innings, leaving him to deal with failure two times out of three! Reason tries to soothe the overwhelming emotional response, reminding you that failure is part of the job, success is just around the corner, etc.

I used to go through a cycle when I was in bad form. It would start with a couple of low scores, something that is easy to cope with and nothing to worry about. But, after another couple, the decline starts. Coaches feel they should do something. Videos are analysed, deficiencies highlighted, remedial action suggested. In the middle, instead of an instinctual reaction to the ball, I'm trying to compensate for the highlighted deficiencies. This usually leads to more failure, more deficiencies. A feeling of helplessness takes over, but this represents the turning point. This is because it's the conscious brain giving up, letting the subconscious take over and do what it does best: react to the ball. Nowadays I try to avoid this deleterious chain of events, but sometimes a trip to the video room becomes inevitable.

Tuesday 29 April

Nottingham

I woke up this morning and had to work out where I was. It feels as if I've hardly slept in my own bed in the last few weeks. Once I got back yesterday, I unpacked, did some laundry and then played a couple of frames of snooker with my house-mate, Rob Ferley. The standard of the verbal battle was far higher than that on the green baize, although we managed to play a couple of half-decent shots by the end.

This morning involved repacking and then driving up to Headingley for nets this afternoon. It promises to be a well-followed game with several England players on show, including the skipper Michael Vaughan.

I spoke to Roger Newman last night, and he reminded me how I had said to him at the start of the year that once I had done my preparation for the season I would back my instinct and take whatever comes. It was a timely reminder as in the last few days I think I have *thought* too much. Time seems to be going so fast that each opportunity takes on such importance. Perhaps I need to relax a little. A nice hundred tomorrow should do the trick…

Wednesday 30 April

Headingley, County Championship – Day One
Yorkshire 51 for one

A rain-affected day. There was a reasonable amount of playing and missing, to be expected in these conditions, but we could only snare one wicket. Hopefully, if we retain the tight lines and lengths we've demonstrated so far, a clutch of wickets will fall when least expected.

Today had the feel of an important game. Geoff Miller, the chief selector, was here. For those of us who haven't played international cricket these games are great opportunities to see what we can do and experience something of the intensity. I was feeling quite nervous and was hoping we would bat so I could get out there and stop worrying. I'm trying not to think too much; I'll just wait and then see what happens.

I'm meeting the boys in the bar tonight to watch the Chelsea–Liverpool game. I have adopted Manchester United as my team. Not that in reality that will mean much as the blanket football coverage has desensitised me to its appeal. Mick, however, is an ardent Liverpool fan so I shall enjoy watching him tonight and perhaps even offering a little of my 'expert knowledge', something bound to rile him!

Thursday 1 May

Headingley, County Championship – Day Two
Yorkshire 299 all out (Swann 4-25, Broad 3-95)
Nottinghamshire 0 for one

Two regulations have come in this year, and both are excellent. The first is that we now play 96 overs in the day, in three sessions of two hours. It may seem trivial, but the 15-minute reduction in those first two sessions has had a sizeable impact on the intensity of the cricket. Today was a perfect example of this. It must have been intriguing cricket to watch as Yorkshire dug in against excellent seam bowling. Ryan Sidebottom, in particular, bowled with great skill for no reward. Graeme Swann took the final four wickets for 25 runs.

The second regulation change is that for every over behind the required rate that a team is at the end of the game they will be deducted one point, an increase from 0.5 points last year. This will have an impact at the end of the season, I'm sure. We were very conscious of being slightly behind for most of the day but caught up with Graeme bowling 15 overs. For a seam-heavy attack such as ours, it will be imperative that we get through our overs as efficiently as possible. It would be truly galling if a tardy over-rate was significant come the end of the season.

Friday 2 May

Headingley, County Championship – Day Three
Yorkshire 299
Nottinghamshire 356 for six (Read 115*, Swann 68, Wagh 56, Broad 52*)

I'm sure Chris Read is fairly bored with his role in the great England wicket-keeper debate. He is the best gloveman in the country, and he is one of the most effective one-day batters on the circuit. Today he showed that he can score well in the longer form of the game with a belligerent hundred. Again, our middle to lower order had contributed heavily to our total: Graeme and Stuart Broad both scoring half centuries.

It appears as though captaincy is bringing out the best in Chris. His keeping has been exemplary, and now it looks as if his batting is firing too. He leads in a different way from Stephen Fleming. He is very consensual, consulting with Mick and Mark Ealham primarily and with the bowlers on the field. Mick has taken a slightly more central position, leading team talks, and is very much in charge off the field. I've mentioned previously how I dislike a dictatorial, we-know-best attitude from management. Well, we have the opposite at the moment. With an experienced motivated bunch of guys, there is no need for anyone to shout and scream.

Saturday 3 May

Headingley, County Championship – Day Four
Yorkshire 299 and 187 for eight (Sidebottom 3-39)
Nottinghamshire 356 for six declared (Read 142, Broad 53)
Match drawn

Sunday 4 May

Trent Bridge, Friends Provident Trophy
Northamptonshire 189 for seven (Pattinson 3-39)
Nottinghamshire 142 for four (Voges 42*, Wagh 26)
Nottinghamshire won by six wickets (by Duckworth-Lewis)

Help from our Down Under this game: Darren with the ball and Adam with the bat. Duckworth-Lewis intervened, but we scraped home to secure a pleasing result. And today I was almost timed out.

Bilal Shafayat had been dismissed whilst I was chatting in the physio's room. I don't tend to watch the cricket if I'm next in, I don't want to get too many preconceived notions of what it will be like, and I want to save my concentration for the middle. When a wicket falls, what normally happens is either a general moan of disappointment from the dressing room lets me know or someone gives me a shout. However, neither of these happened and the first I learned of the wicket was when Mick ran into the room, bearing my helmet and gloves and telling me to get a move on. It was slightly surreal walking out so late after the wicket, frantically strapping on my arm guard, trying to get to the middle as quickly as possible without looking as though I was concerned by the time. I almost ran myself out first ball as well. Just what my reception from Mick would have been sends shivers down my spine even now!

Monday 5 May

A few things to mention. Firstly, it's clear we are playing some good cricket. We almost pulled off an unlikely win at Headingley, taking some late wickets but just running out of time. Yesterday's win (despite Duckworth-Lewis making it a lot tighter than it should have been) was a good performance after 3½ days of hard work

Secondly, volume of cricket. I hope one of the things that has come across reading this diary is that cricket is the central axis of my life. I love playing and the never-ending challenge that it offers. I'd play every day if I could but, as a batter, the work load doesn't affect me in the same way it does a bowler. It's clear that tagging on a one-day game at the end of four days of cricket (and travel), means that the intensity isn't going to be as high as it should be. This doesn't represent a slackening of intent, it just reflects that fact that players are tired. Equally I realise that our job is to entertain the public; it's not for our benefit that the game is in existence. I'm sure that everyone in the entertainment profession gets fatigued from time to time but still has to put on a show. I guess there is always this tension between seeing county cricket as a spectacle for the paying public on the one hand and, on the other, viewing it as an academy for England players.

One of the things that has been on my mind over the last few weeks, buzzing around in the background, is my future in the game. There is so much talk of Twenty20 cricket and, as I'm not sure I'm going to play in our Twenty20 team, it makes me wonder what is going to happen at the end of next year when my contract expires. There are also rumours of us signing another batter. This sounds melodramatic, and for as long as I've played there has always been a threat to my existence as a player. I guess I'll have to cross that bridge at some stage in the future. What is also troubling me a little is that I still have no idea what I'll do if I finish playing the game. I suppose I need to concentrate on the here and now, play good cricket and the rest will follow.

Wednesday 7 May

Trent Bridge, County Championship – Day One
Nottinghamshire 202 all out (Voges 43, Wagh 42)
Kent 33 for four

2.30pm

The conditions are perfect for batting: a great wicket and not a cloud in the sky. However we are not exactly profiting. It nipped around a little this morning as it often does first session. I scored 42 before nicking one to the keeper. This seems to have set the tone for the middle order so far, with Adam and Samit both getting out when set. Once again we need the lower order to help us out.

Later

A fantastic evening session. Ryan Sidebottom took a wicket with the first ball of the innings and we took another three in the final 11 overs of the day. It's a bit of a joke in the dressing room that Ryan only takes wickets for England so he was more than happy with tonight's efforts.

Thursday 8 May

Trent Bridge, County Championship – Day Two
Nottinghamshire 202 & 106 for two (Wood 50, Wagh 21)*
Kent 238 all out (Sidebottom 5-55)

With his huge curly bob of hair, his ferocious presence at the bowling crease and his rampant aggression (occasionally directed at a hapless fielder), you might think Ryan Sidebottom is a fairly nasty man. In fact, his on-field persona is about as far removed from that off it as is possible. He is softly spoken, reluctant to assume the limelight and exceptionally grounded despite his tremendous rise in the international rankings this year.

He has helped to put us in an excellent position. His five wickets were the result of high-quality swing bowling with accuracy, pace and movement all prevalent. It's also a good guide to how much Nottinghamshire cricket means to him; he ran in all day, and at no stage did he look to shirk the mantle of the star bowler.

I only managed 21. Fortunately Matt Wood has played well for a half century to steady the ship. It doesn't take a great deal of savvy to state we will be looking to post a big score tomorrow.

Friday 9 May

Trent Bridge, County Championship – Day Three
Nottinghamshire 202 & 279 all out (Read 88, Wood 58)
Kent 238 & 129 for four

Stuart Broad joined Notts last summer during a meteoric rise to international stardom. It's been difficult to remember he is only 21, such are the levels of expectation. Having bowled relatively poorly in the first innings, and with the media lining him up, he produced an excellent riposte today taking three for 27 off 10 overs. Perhaps it is this ability to turn things around on a sixpence that sets apart the top echelon. There are some parallels between Stuart and a former colleague of mine, Ian Bell. Both were tipped for great things from an early age and indeed were thrust into the fray early on. Ian struggled a little before finding his feet and is now a permanent fixture in the middle order. There are no certainties in sport; indeed to say someone was always going to make it devalues the efforts of that person. It will be fascinating to see how it all turns out.

In this game against Kent we are slightly behind where we would like to be. It's hard to explain why, but on a good wicket in sunny conditions there have been a succession of low scores. The ball has swung at times but not excessively. It's stating the obvious, but we need a couple of our bowlers to produce something special if we are to win.

Saturday 10 May

Trent Bridge, County Championship – Day Four
Nottinghamshire 202 & 279
Kent 238 & 244 for seven
Kent won by three wickets

We didn't have the hoped-for heroics, although Ryan took two wickets in two balls to give us a chance. We were always a wicket behind where we needed to be. It was a quiet dressing room after the game. In cricket, you can see defeat coming from a long way away, it's rare a result takes you by surprise, so reaction can appear muted. The intensity of feeling is spread out over a few hours. At this stage of the season there is no need to check on other results or work out tables, that's all for later; we were just left with that hollow feeling that our hard yakka over three and a half days counted for nothing. Four-day cricket is a great test of endurance, skill and determination. By the end bodies are tired, muscles ache and you feel spent. After a win these are little reminders of mini-battles won, successful performances; in defeat they are just aches and pains.

Sunday 11 May

Trent Bridge, Friends Provident Trophy
Leicestershire 197 all out (Pattinson 4-35, Patel 3-34)
Nottinghamshire 198 for eight (Wood 50, Wagh 37)
Nottinghamshire won by two wickets

Today's game was the complete antithesis of the Kent game. Up to the last couple of balls, three results were possible: tie, win or loss. It was a classic example of almost snatching defeat from the jaws of victory. A fine bowling performance (again), not quite enough runs from the top five (again), and a last gasp effort to get over the line headed by Rob Ferley. At 146 for two, the game was meandering to a tame, uneventful win for us. A benign wicket and a day of beautiful sunshine had had a soporific effect on the crowd and, it would appear, on us. We lost a wicket, then another, then another. Each time we were just about cruising, we hit the self-destruct button. At the end Luke Fletcher, who was so nervous, his mouth so dry that he actually couldn't speak, hit the final ball to extra cover and ran like his life depended on him reaching the other end. Three Leicester players watched as a roll from Boeta Dippenaar passed excruciatingly close to the stumps, followed by a galloping, wide-eyed Fletcher. It was awesome cricket, a hero born. It's often the case that the most entertainment comes when people play poorly or plans go awry.

Mick was seething. He was disappointed with the failure of the top order to see it through. But I was ecstatic. I think the reason our emotions were so different was that having scored some runs, and thus contributed, I was so keen for that contribution to be part of a win, to give value to that effort. That desire to contribute to a win comes with such an overwhelming feeling of accomplishment that the process by which it is achieved becomes irrelevant.

Having had time to reflect, I hope that I haven't antagonised him too much with my reaction. My relationship with Mick is easily the best I've had with a head coach, and it's something I value tremendously.

Monday 12 May

I'm sitting in my local coffee shop. The usual recovery session in the pool this morning, a little physiotherapy on a sore side, now unadulterated sun worshipping. When the weather is like this, the UK is the best place on the planet. Long summer evenings, a glass of wine in the garden, a good book – bliss.

Wednesday 14 May

Trent Bridge, County Championship – Day One
Lancashire 113 all out (Pattinson 6-30) & 4 for no wicket
Nottinghamshire 202 all out (Patel 74, Wagh 55)

Looking at the scores, you might be forgiven for assuming I've missed a day or two diarising. It was an extraordinary day: wickets clearly, but there were also 55 boundaries; it was like a watching a highlights package. Darren Pattinson (six for 30) again bowled superbly, he hasn't bowled a poor spell yet. The wicket has attracted the attention of the pitch inspector. Mick was angry again at our failure to capitalise on the situation by posting a huge score. I don't fully agree; a lead of 90 could be priceless on this wicket. Only time will tell, I guess.

I spoke to Mick about Sunday, and he said he could understand exactly where I was coming from. He said that, since he became a coach, the process rather the outcome was what was important to him, in contrast to how he felt when he was a player. I suppose one of the roles of a coach is to provide emotional balance in a team: remind them of good times when the going is tough and keep feet on ground when we're flying high. By keeping a firm eye on the underlying performance, he can provide little adjustments before they start affecting results.

Thursday 15 May

Trent Bridge, County Championship – Day Two
Lancashire 113 & 233 all out (Shreck 5-40)
Nottinghamshire 202 & 33 for one

It felt as though everyone was waiting. Just what would the pitch do today? Pitch inspectors, umpires, players all holding their breath and waiting. And then … well nothing, actually. The pitch was fine and subsequently received a pass from the inspectors; they must have wondered why they were there as Gary Keedy, the night-watchman, played with a worrying degree of comfort for much of the morning session.

At lunch we weren't in a great position, indeed slightly deflated. We had expected much more from the morning. It was only a two-wicket burst from Paul Franks just on the stroke of lunch that gave us anything to cheer about. Graeme Swann had looked threatening from the Radcliffe Road end, but an inspired move from Chris Read saw Charlie Shreck take over after the break. He swung the ball from good areas and took five for 40 to put us on the verge of another win. It was a great piece of instinctive captaincy. Chris is clearly growing into his role, speaking with greater confidence and projecting an image of someone who is comfortable in his new skin.

Friday 16 May

Trent Bridge, County Championship – Day Three
Lancashire 113 & 233
Nottinghamshire 202 & 147 for three (Voges 69*, Wagh 43*)
Nottinghamshire won by seven wickets

Last night I stubbed my finger, damaging the tendon across the top of my middle finger. So for the next five weeks or so I've got to wear a very annoying splint. It was a freak injury (pulling on my socks, I lost balance, causing the finger stubbing) and obviously moderately embarrassing.

Despite this rather discouraging portent, the cricket today was fantastic. Having lost two wickets in the first over of the day, and with Sunday's near-collapse in the back of our minds, it was a superb challenge. Sajid Mahmood was steaming in, all the Lancashire boys were firing, and Adam Voges and I were both on 0. I went through all the same mental issues: stay still as long as possible, trust that I will have enough time to see the ball, accept any negative thoughts as reminders to do the above. One of the things I've started to take comfort in and use to allay any anxieties is that, if I do stay still, it feels like I have so much more time to make a decision about the ball. In the end we cantered home, Adam playing beautifully for 69 not out off 60 balls. Towards the end I had to fight the demons – the one on my left shoulder was telling me to get it over as quickly as possible, whilst the one on my right was telling me to see it through. It was a satisfying win – we are top of the table and I've met a mini-challenge and played well.

I'm struggling a little as I can't grip properly with my top hand. It seems as though I'm going to have to try just to stroke the ball; any forceful hitting just causes my top hand to come off the bat. Could be a good thing.

Sunday 18 May
Trent Bridge, Friends Provident Trophy
Warwickshire 173 all out (Pattinson 4-29, Patel 3-19)
Nottinghamshire 121 all out (Jefferson 41, Wagh 18)
Warwickshire won by 52 runs

I feel tired, flat, and pissed off having to wear this bloody finger splint. Can't be arsed to write.

Monday 19 May
Yesterday's loss was particularly depressing for a host of reasons. We lost from a position of strength; Warwickshire had just lost to Ireland and so were very low on confidence; and the fact that it was my former team just rubbed salt into the wound. Darren bowled well up front (how many times have I said that?), and we should have cantered home. Instead, Will apart, the batting was poor. There was some decent bowling, but we need to show some resilience and not fall over if we're on the receiving end of a good spell. A thoroughly disappointing day and one to forget as soon as possible.

Tuesday 20 May
Trent Bridge, County Championship – Day One
Sussex 277 all out
Nottinghamshire 46 for two

Wednesday 21 May
Trent Bridge, County Championship – Day Two
Sussex 277 & 70 for two
Nottinghamshire 251 all out (Wagh 54, Voges 53)

A neutral would put Sussex ahead at this stage, and I'd probably agree. However I heard a rumour that both Mushtaq and Lewry are injured, which puts a slightly different gloss to the situation.

I scored 54 today. I wish I knew why I keep getting out in the 50s. Perhaps there is some deep, subconscious self-destruct button. I was lucky to get that many, having been dropped twice last night. This morning, however, I played well. Facing Mushy was a real delight. I couldn't pick his googly and was initially hesitant as a result. So I decided to come down the wicket each time I saw it tossed up. It helped, and I got a few misdirected balls as well. It's an indication of his desire to play for Sussex that he is even appearing in this game. The medical staff apparently thought he should have another week off, but he was determined to play. He is a master of his art, and I was lucky that he was struggling a little today with his knee.

The ball swung consistently all day. It was hard work against their seamers. There is some debate in the changing room as to why wickets are falling so regularly here at Trent Bridge with the new stand and the hover cover being cited. It's undeniable that the scores have been lower than average for both the home and away teams. Chris is keen that we don't expect to be rolled over, as expectation has a nasty habit of becoming fact.

Thursday 22 May

Trent Bridge, County Championship – Day Three
Sussex 277 & 259 all out
Nottinghamshire 251 & 114 for five (Wagh 8)

Relationships are not easy in the best of times, but being away from home regularly exacerbates the difficulties. Being single is both a blessing and a curse. There's a brilliant parody of the motivational poster, with a picture of a man wandering through sand dunes with the by-line, "There might be plenty of fish in the sea, but you're in a desert, alone." It seems to sum up my situation on a too regular basis!

A fellow cricketer and good friend goes into a new relationship with the expectation that it will fail the moment the season starts: once she realises that he will not be around at the weekends, that they won't be able to plan anything during the summer, and then during the winter there's every chance he will be in another country. Absence can make the heart grow fonder, but only for short periods; otherwise it tends to have an ultimately detrimental effect. Of course, that doesn't mean every relationship is doomed to failure, and those that come through the test of a season or two tend to have excellent prognoses.

Friday 23 May

Trent Bridge, County Championship – Day Four
Sussex 277 & 259
Nottinghamshire 251 & 212 (Read 56)
Sussex won by 73 runs

I lost count, but I think we dropped four catches in the second innings. Having dropped more than my fair share over the years, I can empathise. It's the worst feeling in the game: letting down a team mate. Culpable not only for a worsening of the team's position, but also laying to waste the bowler's efforts to that point. We made too many mistakes to win this game; our home ground is not proving to be much of an advantage.

Matt Prior played beautifully in both innings. He had time, composure and balance. There was an inevitability about his innings, as though the most natural conclusion was a hundred. I felt torn between being a player and a spectator: wanting to watch someone so in control of his play but desperately hoping it wouldn't have a harmful effect on the result!

As disappointing as the result was, we had to forget it almost instantly and concentrate on these next three one-day games. We're in Northampton tomorrow (with rain scheduled), back to Trent Bridge on Monday to play Ireland (another dreadful forecast), and at Oakham School to play Leicester on Wednesday. We need to win one, which should allow us to qualify for the quarter-finals.

Sunday 25 May

Northampton, Friends Provident Trophy v Northamptonshire
Rained off

Practice. If you turn up to a game an hour before the start of a day's play, you will see a variety of activity, some prescribed by the coach, other player directed. It is important to differentiate between practice to improve one's skill level and warm up which is intended to put oneself in a state to perform. Practice dominates the off-season, and for me involves volume: lots of balls being hit in an attempt to perfect muscle memory.

During the season, the line between the two becomes blurred as a lack of time means that what should be a warm-up turns into a practice. I'm not sure how much practice is necessary; suggestions often revolve around unhelpful phrases such as "Do as much as you need." I used to hit a lot of balls, believing that if I failed at least I had done all I could in preparation. I remember the former Warwickshire coach John Inverarity telling me to save some of my appetite for the middle, something I didn't really understand at the time. Last year saw me practice much less, I focused on getting a feeling, of waiting until I had assessed the ball and then moving with efficiency into the appropriate shot. And I stopped before I had had enough, at least to my old way of thinking. I wanted to enjoy that feeling of timing a ball but not in practice, I didn't want to satiate my hunger for that feeling in practice. John's words finally hit home.

The only problem is when things aren't going so well. There is always a tendency to practice more, as it's one of the ways we can actually do something. But I wonder sometimes about the mentality behind this. In some ways I see it as a cop out. A 'good attitude' is seen as all-important, occasionally leading to bizarre selections where personality trumps talent. So being seen to put in the hard work, spending extra time in the nets, becomes an end in itself. Then, if failure re-occurs in the middle, the player can feel he's done all he can and is simply unlucky: there's no self-critique, ultimately no honesty. It's as though practice is substituting for the mental strength required for competition.

Of course, this doesn't mean that everyone who practices long and hard is simply doing so for show or lacks the mental ability to step up when it actually matters. But imagine a guy who is viewed as someone who doesn't practice much. He opens himself up to all sorts of personal criticism ("doesn't want it enough", "a slacker", etc); he has to perform otherwise there is nothing for him to fall back on. Now his hunger for success and performance in the middle is the only thing that keeps him in the team. Clearly the best performers in any sport marry copious practice with an ability to bring an X-factor to competition.

I don't have any firm conclusions and the more I write the more questions pop up. Indeed maybe tomorrow I'll have a different view. It seems to me that, despite several years playing the game, I am as confused as I always have been!

Monday 26 May

Trent Bridge, Friends Provident Trophy
Nottinghamshire 241 for six (Voges 82, Patel 75, Read 53, Wagh 10)
Ireland 240 for six
Nottinghamshire won by 1 run

Mixed emotions today. I need to be carefully introspective if I am to be precise. I'm feeling despondent about my performance so far this season. My batting form has been rubbish in the one-dayers and adequate at very best in the four-dayers. Adequate is not a great description actually, inadequate scores hiding behind an average of 47 would be better. My fielding has been poor as well. Not fielding well is an awful feeling – imagine gut-wrenching dread for six hours a day.

I had a good chat with Mick last night. He was heartfelt and honest, expressing frustration with my performance and perplexity at my reactions to getting out. My apparent equanimity in the face of failure is something he couldn't understand. He felt I looked uninterested in the field. He also said I was the best batsman in the side and that I should lead the batting. When he said that, I had this huge surge of appreciation. I felt I was letting him down, and I had a desire to do everything he wanted me to do, as a way of saying thank you for having this faith and belief in me.

All I've been able to think about since is doing well, scoring runs tomorrow, diving and making great saves in the field. I want to convert this will power, this desire to excel, into actual results on the field. I want to dispel this fallacy that I don't care, lack interest. I'd do anything to show people how much I care about my game and that of Nottinghamshire. I've never done the whooping and hollering, and I guess I'm quite laid back, so there are no obvious signs to how much failure hurts or winning matters. And I wish Mick and the rest knew how much I'd love to field well. Actions speak so much louder than words, so every misfield just reinforces the outward impression, leaving any claims to the contrary looking spurious. Yesterday, when I dived over one, I felt humiliation and disgust with myself. And to think that others might think I don't really care just hurts even more.

The game itself was a bit of a wake-up call for us. They needed six to win off the last ball but only managed four. Our innings was almost a replica of the away game: three early wickets, Samit (75) and Adam (82) rebuilding, then Chris (53 not out) adding the finishing touches.

Samit played some lovely shots over extra cover off the spinners. It's a difficult area to defend as the off-side sweeper is often squarer, leaving a big gap to aim for. Nevertheless, there aren't too many batsmen who hit it as well as him. He is ambitious and confident, a good fielder and useful bowler. Runs in the televised Twenty20 games might be enough to push him into contention for an England place.

Adam is a classy batsman. He drives imperiously, defends with the widest bat I've seen and looks very organised. Bizarrely for someone from Perth, he has one of the least tanned bodies in the changing room, only comparable to Chris 'Casper' Read. He's an extremely amiable man and has a very uncomplicated mindset to batting.

It always strikes me how simple the Australian batters I've spoken to keep things: stand there, watch the ball and hit it. A few years ago Brad Hogg was the overseas player at Warwickshire. He averaged 70 at a run a ball that year. I asked him about his pre-delivery movements, something that at the time I was concerned with. Should I go back and across or press with the front foot? Brad just looked blankly at me and said, "I don't know." But surely he must know what he does before the bowler releases the ball? "Not a clue, mate, sorry." I couldn't understand how he didn't know. We spent so long analysing what we were doing, so much thought went into our set-ups, that it seemed vitally important to batting. But, if you watch the best guys, there's virtually no common technique, and what is promoted as poor technique is sometimes the bedrock for someone else.

Technique is important, of course it is. But there comes a point at which it becomes less important than having a belief in your game and a simple objective of hitting the ball. It's funny how aiming to middle every ball causes the rest of your game to fall into place.

Wednesday 28 May

Oakham School, Friends Provident Trophy
Leicestershire 147 for seven (35 overs)
Nottinghamshire 47 for three (12 overs, Wagh 11)
Leicestershire won by 13 runs (by Duckworth-Lewis)

Leicester's innings finished early because of a shower, and then our reply was cut short by a drizzle which turned into persistent rain. Bil Shafayat and I were batting when it rained, at which point we were 15 behind the Duckworth-Lewis target. Against the Leicester opening bowlers, we couldn't get a run: good-length balls bounced up, and we both got pinned trying to hit shorter balls that flew through. So we ended up seeing off the opening bowlers and trying to make up against the second string, knowing that getting out would have made the Duckworth-Lewis situation even worse. The pitch had taken a lot of spin so we were also worried about how to score off their left-arm spinner Claude Henderson. However, just as the second string came on, it started raining, leaving us well behind with nowhere to go (we did eventually get back on for ten balls to try to score 26 which we failed to do).

When we came off, Mick was incandescent with anger, and the rest of the team barely spoke to us. It was a truly awful experience. If we had known that it would rain when it did, and if we had known that their opening bowlers were going to be so miserly for their entire spell, we obviously would have played it differently. We made a decision in real time that didn't work out. In many ways I wish I'd tried to slog one and got out. At least I wouldn't have suffered the post-match fall-out.

Thursday 29 May

It feels like someone is just banging about in my head, hitting me with a hammer, except the hammer is images, feelings, words from yesterday.

I wish it would stop, but my inner world is on constant loop, playing, replaying. It's just killing me.

I can't stand the thought of seeing anyone; I feel like a condemned man, the accused, the wrong-doer. I can hear Mick, see him shaking his head, full of disgust. The feeling of animosity as Bill and I walked off in the rain. Mick's summing up, wanting to get out of the changing room, wanting the car journey to end, just desperate to be on my own.

Self-pity is hardly going to help things, I suppose, and the hurt will fade over the next few days. The correct response is to come out fighting, score runs, field like never before and give Mick the finger, something at the moment I'd love to do. But another part of me just wants to crawl under the duvet, hoping it will all go away.

Not sure what I'm going to do today. Probably gym at some stage, coffee somewhere. Write a bit more. Meet Miss Perfect. Give up the game. One of the aspects of myself I like least is a desire for sympathy when things have gone wrong. So I start thinking of things I could do: retirement, jumping out of windows, etc, that would garner sympathy. I hate it, yet it's there. Sympathy seeker, pathetic.

Monday 2 June

It is so easy to say all those pop psychology phrases that are supposedly the precursor to success. Mental toughness is child's play; courage, belief, no problem. Just look up on the internet, find appropriate language and there you are. I am, however, a walking example of someone for whom it is becoming very hard work to fake the part. It disheartens me a little, putting that hitherto nebulous thought into words. Practice today is something I am definitely not looking forward to, and the trip to Durham (if I make it, far from a certainty) will just be a reminder of that awful day last week.

Whatever you do, don't think of a pink elephant with huge ears! What are you thinking about? Exactly. Just substitute 'any negative thoughts or beliefs' for the pachyderm and that is supposedly the recipe for success: you will be the person you think you are. Damn!

There is some hope however. There's only one way to go from the rocky bottom.

The season so far

County Championship – Division One

Canterbury	Kent	52		Won by 10 wickets
Headingley	Yorkshire	56		Drawn
Trent Bridge	Kent	42	21	Lost by 3 wickets
Trent Bridge	Lancashire	55	43*	Won by 7 wickets
Trent Bridge	Sussex	54	8	Lost by 73 runs

Table on 3 June

	P	W	L	D	Pts
Somerset	5	2	-	3	67
Sussex	6	1	1	4	59
Nottinghamshire	5	2	2	1	58
Surrey	6	-	1	5	55
Durham	4	2	1	1	53
Yorkshire	5	1	1	3	53
Kent	5	1	2	2	46
Lancashire	5	1	1	3	46
Hampshire	5	-	1	4	39

Friends Provident Trophy – Midland Group

Edgbaston	Warwickshire	-	Abandoned
Dublin	Ireland	0	Won by 56 runs
Trent Bridge	Northamptonshire	26	Won by 6 wickets
Trent Bridge	Leicestershire	37	Won by 2 wickets
Trent Bridge	Warwickshire	18	Lost by 52 runs
Northampton	Northamptonshire	-	Abandoned
Trent Bridge	Ireland	10	Won by 1 run
Oakham	Leicestershire	11	Lost by 13 runs

Final table

	W	L	A	Pts
Leicestershire	5	2	1	11
Nottinghamshire	4	2	2	10
Northamptonshire	4	2	2	10
Warwickshire	2	4	2	6
Ireland	1	6	1	3

Chapter Seven

Reflections

Reading through the diary so far, there is an obvious drift from pre-season optimism to the tougher realities of the season. Batting hasn't been easy and, with the bowlers doing well, there has been added pressure on the batting unit.

I can't believe that it was only a few months ago I was in Uganda. Reading the entries brought back how much fun it was out there, but it feels as if it happened to someone else. Time is like an accordion: sometimes compressed, as in the middle of a game; other times elongated. The times between events can seem like aeons.

As a team, our cricket has been good. Third in the Championship and well placed in the Friends Provident. I'm playing well in the former and poorly in the latter. Given the generally low scores, I'm pleased that I am consistent even if I haven't nailed the 'big' scores.

I've also been struck by the intensity of emotion that I've recorded. I suppose writing a diary there is a bound to be a tendency to focus on the big emotions. It would be rather dull if I just said I was OK all of the time. I also think that I have a leaning to over-emphasise the negative aspects in this diary and play down any positive emotions. I think that in reality I am more balanced than has come across so far. But does this emphasis on the negative confirm that I am indeed mentally weak? I can imagine the 'tough' cricketer rubbishing some of my reactions to events.

We are emotional creatures. Emotions evolved because they aid survival; they are useful. For me, whatever a person's emotional reaction is, what is crucial is how that person subsequently acts. Let me illustrate with a hypothetical example. Two cricketers, Bert and Bruce, both experience exactly the same event: they bag a pair in their first county game. Bert, brought up to believe it's un-masculine to show emotion, just scowls and barely utters a word. Bruce, on the other hand, is clearly distraught, holding his head in his hands, perhaps even a tear in the corner of the eye.

Now, is Bert mentally stronger than Bruce? Their initial emotional responses are irrelevant for me; what matters is how they use their differing reactions. Does Bruce convert his despair into solid determination or does he crumble at the first thought of failure? Is Bert's refusal to show disappointment just a symptom of someone unable to accept help from other people? Or is he so confident in his abilities that a failure has no effect?

It is possible that both Bruce and Bert will turn up in exactly the same state of mind for the next game: equally focused and determined. They have just arrived there by different routes. I can understand coaches favouring those who choose one particular route over the other, as everyone understands people who are similar to themselves. But both Bruce and Bert would bring equally valuable qualities to their team.

Of course, this is a simplified situation and reality is rarely so clean cut: people are not so either/or. But, if we think a little beyond the obvious, there is a whole lot more going on that requires consideration.

Chapter Eight

June and early July

Tuesday 3 June

I'm trying to put off packing. I'm in bed reading *Captain Corelli's Mandolin*. I've got the new James Bond book by Sebastian Faulks waiting, so as much as I'm enjoying my present read I can't wait to get started on the next. I read *The Reluctant Fundamentalist* by Mohsin Hamed last week. The quality and precision of the writing was extraordinary and certainly throws my meagre efforts into stark relief.

We are travelling up to Durham for tomorrow's quarter final, the biggest game of the year so far. It is raining now, but it is forecast to be fine for the game. They are an excellent team. I remember their entry to the first-class game in 1992 when they were the whipping boys. How times have changed!

5.30pm

Arrived late at the ground, relations with Mick frosty at best. A few throw downs with him though and while slightly tense we got through. Heavy rain all day. No one wants to see this going into a second day so hopefully all the work the ground staff were doing with the super-soppers will pay off.

Wednesday 4 June

Chester-le-Street, Friends Provident Trophy – Quarter Final
Nottinghamshire 188 all out (Patel 114, Wagh 3)
Durham 189 for nine (Patel 3-27)
Durham won by one wicket

An extraordinary innings from Samit Patel (114) gave us half a chance, and a stupendous display with the ball almost got us home. When they were 127 for one, we were resigned to defeat, but then Samit came up trumps with the ball this time (3-27) and a collapse ensued. Only a fine innings from Gareth Breese prevented us from getting through to the semis.

It was Samit's maiden one-day hundred, and it was a fantastic illustration of what he can do: superb strikes over mid-on, mid-off and – his trade mark area – extra cover, played with a shoulder-rolling, Viv Richards-esque confidence. He has been excellent in this competition, and it's a shame that he won't get the chance to parade his talents in a Lord's final.

It was unsurprisingly a quiet dressing room after the game. I think everyone realises that our season is at an important fulcrum. The top order again failed in this game and is an ongoing concern and, with the Championship so close and competitive, we can't afford to slip up.

Thursday 5 June

Mum is a very keen gardener, and today she is working in my garden. She and Dad first met in the offices of Hartland Tidd and Co in 1972, a small estate agency in Harborne where she was a secretary and dad was looking for a place to rent. They married in 1975, I was born in October of the following year, and my sister, Claire, followed me in March 1979. Dad was a supply teacher and worked in the comprehensive schools throughout Birmingham. He was born in Bombay and had come across to UK in 1968. When compared to his naturally conservative character, this leap into the unknown seems atypical, but Dad had a love of travelling, something he shares with Mum, and I guess this was another adventure.

Any pressure I felt growing up was, I think, self-generated. Mum and Dad were both concerned that I did well, but they certainly weren't the pushy, off-spring promoting, denizens of the rugby touchline. At one stage, when I was 14 or so, I remember experiencing a particularly bad trot in the school team, I had accumulated the Audi rings – four noughts in a row. Dad was fairly worried to say the least, and he spoke to Roger about it. Roger said that the best thing he could do was to not turn up, give me some space, and that he was going to promote me to opener until I scored some runs. It must have been a bitter pill to swallow, but he did, and it worked – I scored a hundred in the next game. Funnily enough, I feel more pressure from them now than I did back then. I can sense their worry from the stands, but it does make any runs I score when they are there doubly sweet.

My motivation over the years has evolved. I suppose when I first started I simply enjoyed doing something I was good at. But, as I got into the youth system, I became focussed on team selections and making progress towards the holy grail of a professional contract. I now feel ambivalent about a highly structured system for young cricketers. On the one hand, the coaching and opportunities I received to advance my game were undoubtedly beneficial, but on the other I feel that a less regimented environment, one where I concentrated on the enjoyment of the game rather than purely the outcome, could have been more helpful to me in some ways. Once I became a professional, playing for England became my raison d'être, I tried to train harder than everyone else, hoping to achieve success through pure slog. I felt that I deserved to do well, purely because of the hours I put in. After 2005, when I suffered what could have been a career-ending injury, I realised that the likelihood of representing England was fading quickly and that I should be grateful for each day on the cricket field. This was sorely tested in the following season, but it is an ethos in which I firmly believe. Now I see each day as an opportunity to discover more of what I can achieve, valuing my time in the game. During 2007 I continually surprised myself; I actually started to enjoy the uncertainty each day brought.

But motivation isn't a single-stringed instrument. At Oxford the sponsors provided a bottle of champagne for our man of the match, and it became a goal to collect as many as possible. I've also felt the presence of former coaches urging me on, and a keen sense that I had let them down if I failed. Then there is personal pride, both in my own performance and that of my team. Returning to Warwickshire last year, I was struck by how much I wanted my new set of team-mates to impress on my old stomping ground.

Friday 6 June

Old Trafford, County Championship – Day One
Lancashire 260 for five

Body feeling sore this evening after another long car journey yesterday and a lot of running on the hard Old Trafford surface today. My knees feel like they are about twice the age of the rest of my body!

Charlie Shreck has extended his contract for another two years. I hope he got a great deal because he is one of the best bowlers in the country and also one of the most amiable, decent men on the circuit. That view might not have been shared by the Lancashire batsmen today, as he snarled and growled his way to a verbal warning from the umpires. He is an old-fashioned, aggressive fast bowler who enjoys nothing more than bowling his heart out and taking wickets. He has phenomenal stamina and the ability to bowl match-winning spells. He is a real asset to the club.

Although we only took five wickets today we have kept on top of the run rate so they are not running away with the game. It's a good wicket, not as fast as we thought it would be, but it might take some spin later in the game. Unless one team bats badly it's going to be difficult to force a result.

Saturday 7 June

Old Trafford, County Championship – Day Two
Lancashire 384 all out
Nottinghamshire 148 for two (Wagh 67*)

I played well today, feeling in control. It is an excellent surface, abrasive to the ball but with true bounce and consistent pace. On pitches like these, the overriding thought is one of making sure you don't miss out. We need to post a big total and score relatively quickly as we will need to time to take ten wickets.

It's always a pleasant feeling to walk off at the end of the day not out. It extends the warm glow of accomplishment associated with a decent knock just that bit longer.

Sunday 8 June

Old Trafford, County Championship – Day Three
Lancashire 384 & 146 for four
Nottinghamshire 304 all out (Wagh 94, Voges 55)

A pretty dismal day: out in the 90s, we fail to nail a big score and also can't bag any more than four wickets. It's been a physically tough game so far. I've mentioned the hard surface, and cricket always seems harder if you're not taking regular wickets.

Monday 9 June

Old Trafford, County Championship – Day Four
Lancashire 384 & 234 for six, declared
Nottinghamshire 304 & 178 for four (Read 71*, Franks 42, Wagh 0)
Match Drawn

A tame draw. Gutted to miss out in the second innings, caught down the legside. Exhausted, now having driven back. Mark Ealham was my travel partner for this trip, and he helped pass the hours in the car. Can't wait to sleep ...

Wednesday 11 June

Twenty20 practice at the ground, the nets resembling a golf driving range. Chris Cairns was next to me, which was like a tank alongside a pea-shooter. Mick spoke to me and said I'm unlikely to figure in the competition, barring Chris's registration not going through or injury/loss of form. I'm not sure how I feel about that; it's certainly something I was expecting and, to be honest, agree with. We have some excellent strikers of the ball, and I'm not sure if I'd be any good.

The upside is that I get a couple of weeks to relax and go to the gym. It might seem odd that I'm not more upset about missing out. But I just don't see the point of getting too worked up. I might end up playing anyway, as I did last year. What's the point of wasting time and effort getting angry over something I don't really have any control over?

Well, that is the positive gloss. Not playing is pretty awful. From being at the centre of the batting effort I'm relegated to the sidelines. The thrills and spills of the games, the banter in the changing room, the sense of togetherness, will all be lost to me. For periods during my time at Warwickshire, I was playing the four-day games but not the one-dayers. It's a horrible feeling to have to pack your kit on the last day of a championship game to make way for someone else. It's exacerbated by the fact that emotions can run on overdrive in limited-overs cricket, forging real team spirit of which I'm not a part. Returning to the fold a couple of days later, it feels like you've missed out on something and so, just slightly, you are on the outside.

Thursday 12 June

If there was a point at which I had to choose cricket over any other profession, it was at university. In my final year, my friends were doing the milk rounds, going to interviews, trying to decide into which area of corporate life they were going to plunge. I remember feeling like a bystander in this swirling tide of decisions, prospects and uncertainty.

Cricket offers a wonderful life but, just when my cohorts would be cashing in on the hard work in their 30s, I would be looking for a new job. So, having made the "decision" to be a cricketer, I have always had this little demon on my shoulder, asking me what I'm going to do when I finish playing the game. In my first few years he was shouting fairly loudly, so during the winters I worked in the computer department at Pertemps Recruitment and then at stockbrokers Williams de Broe. But I decided that, if I was going to be the best cricketer I could be, I should devote the off season to training and playing. It was also an attempt to bury my head firmly in the sand, as I couldn't think of any profession which energised me in the same way cricket did. I still have no clue as to what I would do if cricket finished tomorrow. I enjoy writing and I enjoy trading (stock markets, although if you want a tip, doing the exact opposite of what I do should make you a few quid), so perhaps the final solution lies in those realms.

If I tell someone I meet that I play cricket, there follows with absolute certainty two questions: "Does it pay well?" (usually asked with a look which says, "You poor soul, you must be eating baked beans everyday") and "What do you do in the winters?" The second opens a line of conversation more interesting than the first, so I tend to focus on that.

Amongst other things I have played cricket in South Africa and Australia, learned tango in Buenos Aires and trekked to Everest base camp. I'm very fortunate in that for five months of the year I can do pretty much whatever I please, as long as it contributes to making me the best I can be. It can be a double-edged sword, though, as having nothing to do beyond gym and nets can become insanely repetitive. Work and obligations give a day structure and meaning; without it lethargy and boredom can take over. I'm aware that for the majority of the population such gripes are unlikely to find a sympathetic audience, and possibly rightly so. I love being a cricketer and wouldn't want to do anything else, but because the summers are so charged with emotion and consequence, sometimes the winters can seem dull and tedious by comparison.

Monday 16 June

The boys are two wins from two in the T20. We look very strong. We have so many people who can clear the rope with the bat and bowlers who can take wickets up front and bowl 'block hole' at the death. And we're doing this without Graeme Swann who will be available for the later rounds. My house mate Rob Ferley performed well in the last game against Durham, taking three for 17 off his four overs. He is in his last year of contract and needs to impress during these two weeks whilst Graeme is away. With the increasing importance of T20, players like Rob who may not play every game during the season but develop into dependable performers in this form are going to become ever more valuable to counties. He is philosophical about success in this competition, knowing that he could bowl as well as he did on Saturday but get smashed around the park in the next game. It's certainly true that, in such short spells, one or two hits either way can make a huge difference.

Wednesday 18 June

I don't watch too much television but I do like *Big Brother*. I wonder if I get the same reaction when I mention this as other fans do. The other person immediately assumes the televisual high ground, expressing almost personal offence that anyone tunes in to such rubbish. I defend my choice a little and the qualities of the programme. Then something strange happens: as I talk about the show, the other person starts to join in, admits to watching a bit "when the girlfriend's got the TV on." It's as though they feel that they should establish that they are not the sort to watch such drivel and in no way resemble the sort that do. But once that is understood, then they seem happy to admit to hours of happy viewing.

One of the aspects of BB living that interests me is the value the house mates put on 'genuineness' and their dislike of 'two-facedness'. The house mates feel one should always give one's evaluation of the personality and behaviour directly to the person concerned. My issue with this is that my opinions of people are changing all the time; I can go from one end of the spectrum to another within the space of a few hours. This diary is testament to the transitory nature of feelings and beliefs; it might require a constant commentary to avoid the crime. Also, the effect of being disliked is asymmetrical to that of being liked, so a momentary dislike can weigh heavily on the relationship.

In the dressing room, where we are all pushing towards a common goal, these temporary (or even permanent) likes/dislikes are almost irrelevant. Two-facedness in this case is a sensible strategy, by which I mean ignoring those transitory feelings or at least sitting on them for a while. Honesty is often cited as a quality people value most in others. True no doubt in our most important relationships, but not necessarily so in the majority of everyday interactions. Some form of pragmatism is required, in which sensitivity and intelligence decide the degree to which honesty prevails.

Thursday 19 June

Our T20 progress hit a speed bump in the form of Derbyshire on Tuesday, and the group remains tight. Tonight's game is against Leicester. There's a reasonable amount of rivalry between the teams, with a collection of personal duels over the last few years adding extra spice to the contest.

My current book, *The Black Swan* by Nassim Taleb, is, along with the *God Delusion* by Richard Dawkins, on my (very short) list of books that everyone should read. Taleb is an exceptional thinker and there seems to be a revelation on every page. One of his ideas is that, in order to know what produces success, we shouldn't just review the characteristics of the successful but look at the failures too. He asserts that many of the qualities that are supposedly drivers of success are also shared by the failures; it's just that their stories never get written. He feels we underestimate the impact of luck.

As I read this, I couldn't help but smile to myself. So much of a sportsman's mentality is based around the idea that he is in control of his destiny. From an early age, the influence of luck is downplayed and his ability to control events emphasised. I've often thought that there's a large group of people who could have been successful cricketers but for one reason or another didn't get a break at the right time. Obviously the exceptionally talented have a far greater chance of rising to the top, but I'm not sure there is an enormous gulf between 90% of county cricketers and some of the people who have fallen by the wayside.

Friday 20 June

I spent the afternoon in Lincoln at an Asda Kwik Cricket day. Schools from around the county were competing to be in the finals to be held at Trent Bridge in September. Some of the kids were Notts fans and so asked for an autograph. This had an interesting effects as other children could see what was going on, didn't know who I was but thought it best to play safe and join in, just in case I was a footballer/pop star. Children were clamouring to get something signed, delighted to get my written moniker, but then slightly confused and uncertain when they realised that they still didn't know what it was they had collected. Nevertheless, demand spiralled and in the end my autograph became quite sought after. It gave me a perfect example of the dynamics of the art market.

One aspect of the day of which I'm not particularly proud is that lots of the kids wanted to know why I wasn't playing. Rather than simply saying I wasn't picked, my ego kicked in and I hid behind my finger injury.

Saturday 21 June

It's grey, dank and mizzling, a reflection of my mood. Another win in the T20 yesterday brought bittersweet emotions: pleased for the guys, but it signals the final nail for any hopes I may have had of playing in this competition. I'm also concerned that I may not play in the Pro40, especially as Graeme will be available. It's frustrating, annoying, depressing, maddening, but ultimately it's my helplessness that's hardest to deal with.

Will Jefferson scored 42. He has struggled this year but is playing well in this competition, the requirement for positive strokeplay resolving any uncertainty in his game. Mick considers Will to be the most talented player he has seen since Kevin Pietersen, quite an accolade.

Each day this week I've done a gym session and some work with Paul Johnson on the bowling machine, both of which have been useful and enjoyable. It's like a mini mid-season break, and fortunately this is also the final week of having to wear this splint on my finger. A ray of sunlight in a bleak landscape.

Sunday 22 June

A loss to Lancashire has opened up the group, making qualification, like so many of these games, something that will go down to the wire. I feel very confused when thinking about the mechanics of T20 cricket and what makes a good player/team. I'm sure there is a good mathematical model which can predict which teams will triumph and which qualities are sought after (although having read *The Black Swan* I would be tremendously suspicious of such a model). We love to be able to explain, often fitting the past around our beliefs. I look at our team and, as I have said, I can't really see a weakness. So how can we lose?

Perhaps the differences between teams aren't that great. Perhaps cricket is not based around simple probability. Perhaps the ability to get a team to achieve its potential is itself subject to complex, interdependent probabilities. Perhaps luck has a bigger say than we care to admit?

I feel like ranting: the result of a couple of glasses of wine and several helpings of anger. Watching the game today, I was fucked off that I wasn't given the opportunity to play, I know I can play shots that could win us games, I'm being denied the chance to experience the unique excitement of this game and to help my county win games. And without wanting to sound too arrogant, I was the Player of the Year last year, so you might think that I would feature as one of our best batters.

This isn't helping, I'm just getting more angry, I feel like hurling the fucking keyboard through the window.

Later

Rob can't understand why it's taken me so long to get this angry. I think initially I agreed with their decision. Now I realise I can do what a good batsman needs to do in T20.

Monday 23 June

Mick said I was dressed like Jason Gallian so I promptly took myself off to Diesel to halt my decline into the middle-class, check-shirt-with-cords, sartorial wasteland.

I've got to run drinks around for the next few games. Part of the job, but slightly demeaning nonetheless. It's difficult to feel (one of) the best batsmen in the team when acting as a waiter.

Good banter with Wayne Noon this morning. We often try to enliven throw downs by inventing scenarios, pitting him against me. This time, on a terrible wicket, I had to score six an over without getting out. We adopted tennis scoring as Wimbledon starts this week: each over I succeeded was a game to me, and vice versa. He won 6-5, which was a blessing as neither of us was keen for a tie break.

The physio's room was quite busy: I took my splint off and started to mobilise the joint (painful, but so pleased); Chris Cairns was having some ultrasound on a creaky knee; Darren Pattinson was having his dislocated finger soothed; and Will Jefferson popped in to ice his hands. From this stage of the season it will be a case of just keeping people together long enough to get through; niggles and strains, a natural consequence of playing, just don't have enough time to heal fully.

Tuesday 24 June

We've lost to Leicester, failing to chase down 131. I was running drinks. A dressing down from Mick after the game (funnily, even though I clearly had no culpability, I felt chastised) and general despondency. We're not out of the competition yet but need a result from the last two games at least. In the end, on a personal level, today wasn't too bad. I enjoyed the warm-ups, beating fitness coach Kevin Paxton (ex-semi pro footballer) in a game of football tennis. I could watch Kev for hours, his every mannerism makes me laugh, from the express pace of his walking to the intensity of concentration when doing a Sudoku. I've found myself seeking him out – truly excellent company.

Wednesday 25 June

I'm on a coach heading up to Old Trafford. In a selectoral volte face, I'm a member of the squad for the game against Lancashire. I'm not sure I'll end up playing, but I practised some hitting/slogging on the bowling machine just in case.

Later

I'm not playing. It's funny, but I could see the same look on the other two left out: in our heads we have all the reasons we should be playing, and writ large across our faces are disappointment and resentment. Selection is prediction: who will perform best in the near future. It's possible to make a case for or against most people which makes arguing futile. In fact, it just entrenches positions. I argue why I should play, the coach justifies his decision by telling you how bad you are – great! At the end of the day, management are paid to make these decisions and must be accountable for them.

Later still

We lost, fairly easily in the end. I'm starting to wonder how bad the selectors must think I am in this form of the game. Perhaps I'll sneak in on Friday as a wild card. That sense of goodwill I felt towards Mick a few weeks ago is rapidly evaporating. It's not a particularly mature reaction, 'slightly petulant child' now I come to think of it, but I really value loyalty. And I think you should back your best players. It's probably fair to say that I'm not dealing with this particular aspect of professional sport very well. Part of me is glad we've lost. I know that is professional heresy, but that's my raw unedited emotional reaction. I guess tomorrow and over the next few days this anger will subside, but it leaves a nasty aftertaste. I even got a bit tetchy with Mark Ealham on the bus. I'm really taking not playing too personally.

I know what it is like to be on the other side. As captain at Oxford, I was always grateful when those who didn't make the team remained upbeat and helpful, not self-concerned and morose. There's another part of my psyche that I am barely acknowledging even to myself: in a little corner of my mind I'm glad that I'm not playing. When I wake up on a match day, the first emotion that greets me, before there's a chance for the rest of my mind to react, is anxiety. It quickly recedes, but it takes effort. Being in the spotlight is taxing, and to be on the sidelines is easy. I can tell myself what a great player I am, that I would have performed so well given half a chance, without the litmus test of a game.

Over the last couple of days, I've started to think about the weekend and playing in the championship game. I oscillate between a violent desire to prove them wrong and apathetic surrender. It will be interesting to see how I go.

Thursday 26 June

Excellent chat with my agent Darren Long. I got a lot of stuff off my chest: my inability to marry being told I was the best batter with my not playing despite the fact that we are batting so badly; the feelings of frustration; the hurt at feeling let down by selectors. The silver lining is the realisation that I am good enough to play this game: at last, self belief.

Darren pointed out that what happens from here is up to me. I can let this fester or I can look back at the end of the season and see it as a storm in a tea cup. I wrote down a few thoughts. The most important things are two goals: to be one of the top five batters in the country and to be Nottinghamshire's Player of the Year 2008.

Friday 27 June

There are two very distinct versions of Mick: a dustbin-kicking, angry, irritable one usually seen during cricket matches, and a reasonable, amiable, wouldn't-mind-having-a-pint-with-him one. It's virtually impossible to feel any anger or malevolent feelings towards the latter, and that was the version that was at practice today. He had texted me last night, saying I was inked in for the Pro40 side, and all the vitriolic seething inside of me dissipated. I need that to happen because otherwise this situation (which I'm going to try to avoid mentioning again) could take over.

We practised hitting over the top on the bowling machine. I hit them pretty well, perhaps a tiny point proved.

Saturday 28 June

Down in Southampton. The usual procedure for these away games is that we get to the ground the day before and do a couple of hours' practice. I enjoy these sessions; they always start with a game of football and then revolve around whatever each player needs. I tend to do some fielding and some throw downs, whilst others like Samit and Adam Voges will have a net. I mentioned a silver lining from the last couple of weeks is a new-found focus and determination. I really felt this today and had to remind myself that I should expend this energy in the game as I could have practised for another couple of hours.

Adam was helpful in passing on a couple of fielding tips, and I made a couple of suggestions to Charlie Shreck about his batting. I like working with the tail-enders and hopefully I was some use.

Hampshire are a good side although Shane Warne, who has been talismanic for them over the last few seasons, is a huge loss. It will be interesting to see how they are coping without him. I've mentioned his magical ability to make good players excellent, and somehow to get his team over the finishing line. Playing against him is always fun because he is constantly trying something, whether it is through field settings or when he is bowling himself.

We are waiting on the fitness of Graeme Swann who has a problem with his elbow. He was playing in England's defeat by New Zealand in the decisive fifth ODI. The boys reckon he just fancies a night in London, but I can't believe that of our Graeme ...

A more interesting selection decision involves Mark Ealham. It appears he isn't playing because he needs to rest, something I can't quite work out as we have nine days off after this fixture. If Swanny doesn't play, Mark is our main source of control on the field, rarely going at over three an over. It's fortunate that we have Andre Adams to step in. He showed last year that he is a quality performer, and he will be keen to make an impression straight away.

Sunday 29 June
Southampton, County Championship – Day One
Hampshire 293 all out (Adams 4-63)
Nottinghamshire 13 for no wicket

An excellent day's cricket. Looked like it was going to be a very long one after the first hour. The pitch was slow with not a lot of assistance for the seamers. In what was an inspired selection move (!), Andre bowled beautifully, taking four wickets and starting the rot amongst the Hampshire batters.

I loved being back in the thick of things. Made me appreciate being a cricketer. It was great running around in the field, and I fielded well; it felt fantastic to be part of a good team and doing my bit in the field.

Monday 30 June
Southampton, County Championship – Day Two
Hampshire 293
Nottinghamshire 337 for seven (Wood 77, Wagh 66, Voges 49)

Before play started, Mick spoke about making sure they were fielding tomorrow morning and seeing how they shape up after a day in the field. Well, that objective was reached so we are very pleased. I put on 149 with Matt Wood, who played well for 77. Vogesy got 49 as well. I feel good about this because, with three out of the top five making scores, it feels like we made a contribution as a unit. We've let down the bowlers too many times, after they have worked so hard to get the opposition out. It hasn't always been easy but, when today Andre said he appreciated that the batters had laid a foundation for his hitting this evening, I felt delighted.

Woody has struggled up till now. Coming from the wickets at Taunton to those at Trent Bridge is bound to take some getting used to. He plays with languid ease, timing balls with a slow swing and gentle touch of the bat. He is a quiet achiever, having already captained his county and reaching level four in his coaching qualifications.

On a personal note I was happy to get 66, given that I was dropped on 0. It seemed a decent ball which I nicked to slip who kindly dropped it. It just shows how much luck is involved in the game. Batting was quite hard work on this wicket, always a little something there but not much pace to work with. Nevertheless I was very disappointed to get out: I'm not going to fulfil my new targets if I don't cash in and get some big runs.

The mood in the camp this evening was good. We had a team meal organised by Adam Voges. He's a thoroughly good guy, and I hope we see more of him next year. As for prospects, if we can get a bit of a lead we've got a chance of a result as the ball has 'nibbled' off the pitch a little. We'll have to bowl well to get ten wickets, but that's what we've been doing all year.

Tuesday 1 July
Southampton, County Championship – Day Three
Hampshire 293 & 248 all out (Adams 4-45)
Nottinghamshire 354 all out & 54 for one (Wagh 27*)

Wednesday 2 July
Southampton, County Championship – Day Four
Hampshire 293 & 248
Nottinghamshire 354 & 189 for four (Wagh 67, Patel 65*)
Nottinghamshire won by six wickets

Mid-afternoon

I am intensely bored, the dribble that is masquerading as play-stopping rain continues and I've exhausted all the usual distractions: newspapers, crosswords, music, book. I did hear of an interesting and, as far as I am aware, novel rain-break activity – a banana speed-eating competition. During a stoppage in the second-team game last week, three of the guys lined up three bananas and on the whistle tried to see them off as quickly as possible. Alex Hales won in a time of 53 seconds. Brilliant.

Later

We won despite having to wait a couple of hours for the rain to clear. Samit played his way to a good 65 not out, taking the game away from Hampshire if there was any lingering doubt when he came to the wicket. I chipped in with 67 and played as well as I have for a while. I was middling a lot of my defensive shots which tells me I was watching the ball for longer. The work I've done with Paul Johnson has definitely helped, and I'm going to book in for some more sessions over the next few days.

The bowlers were excellent down here, and the middle order has fired as well.

Thursday 3 July

Recovery this morning was performed with a chorus of complaint. Why were we having this session when most people hadn't done anything yesterday? I think it was a fair point, but we did some swimming which I like so I wasn't too peeved.

We've got the next few days off, back in on Tuesday. A few have taken this opportunity to take a mini-holiday; Charlie Shreck has returned to his roots in Cornwall; Darren Pattinson is in Ireland; and Chris Read is beautifying for a couple of days in a spa!

In some ways I want to keep playing. But I'll use this time for some gym and more Johnno bowling machine sessions. This apparently laudable activity is just the result of having nothing else to do. One of the autograph hunters took a picture of me, and I was shocked at how much weight I'd put on. If I needed extra motivation, Jamil is getting married in October on a beach in the Seychelles. In my present state I'll have conservation groups throwing water over me and trying to get me back into the sea.

Friday 4 July

We are top of the table. It's tight, and there is a long way to go. I think Durham are a key side, and we will need two solid results against them. I'm averaging 50 which I'm pretty happy about.

I spent this morning trawling the charity shops looking for a 'cheap suit and shades' – the dress code for a team event at the races next Tuesday.

Wednesday 9 July

It looks like we have been given a life line in the T20 – Yorkshire may have cocked up a registration of one the players who took the field against us in the crucial group game at TB a few weeks ago. Rob Ferley just kept repeating "gold dust, it's absolute gold dust" as the drama unfolded on Monday. Mick seems to think that the most likely outcome of the hearing tomorrow is a replay of our game and the winners playing Durham. Name on the trophy?

Training this morning was very funny. Most of the guys sported Olympic hangovers from last night's team event at the races, and probably the last thing any of them wanted was a net followed by some circuits. It provided great entertainment, especially when one of our fast bowlers, looking decidedly queasy, felt it was prudent to remain hovering by the door, just in case a dash to the loo was required.

Last night was a huge success. The guys love any opportunity to dress up in fancy dress, and there were some superb outfits. Darren Pattinson had found a suit someone had died in, Mark Footitt looked like Micky from *Only Fools and Horses*, and Graeme Swann was straight from the set of *Miami Vice*. Unfortunately, Mark Ealham had a different sense of a 'cheap suit' and was, wearing one he paid £400 for about ten years ago. It was pointed out that a) not only was that not cheap by today's standards but, b) accounting for inflation over the intervening decade, it was probably worth several thousand pounds (maths at this time of night was not an exact science). He claimed to have had it 'valued' at £18.50, an argument that fell on deaf ears.

Thursday 10 July

After practice this morning I drove down to Edgbaston to commentate on the T20 quarter final against Kent for Radio 5 Live. I enjoyed it; I think given half a chance it's something I'd like to do more of. After the game I did ten minutes on Darren Gough's show. It had just been announced that Yorkshire are disqualified from the competition. Apparently they were aware of problems with Azeem Rafiq's registration last year but had done nothing about it. Yorkshire are planning to appeal, Durham aren't happy and the whole situation is messy with no one coming out with much credit. Goughy was irate, and I sympathised. They had to come to TB and win to go through, something they did easily. Yet, through no fault of their own, they won't be playing in the semis. And of course the turmoil in Azeem's life now must be awful. I said that the only silver lining might be a discussion within the game about the nature of Kolpaks, overseas, locals, EU and the myriad routes to qualification within the game. It has been going on without any real resolution for a while now, so maybe this debacle will catalyse the process.

I'm heading off to bed as I've got an early alarm call. I want to get a 3G iPhone tomorrow, but it looks as if I'm going to have to get to the shop first thing to have any chance. There's a fair amount of rain around so I'm gambling that I'll get some time for a bit of a kip during the day. Rational argument goes out the window, though, when it comes to Apple products – it's all in the heart!

Friday 11 July

Trent Bridge, County Championship – Day One
Surrey 59 for two

4.30 a.m.: can't sleep (feels just like Christmas morning), and hate the thought of wasting an hour in bed when the queues could be forming. Check the forecast – bugger, heavy showers have turned into light rain at best. Too late to change my mind, though. Drive into town, completely deserted, just hope there isn't a huge queue already.

It's 5.15 and I turn the corner to see … a tramp huddled under a blanket sitting on a piece of cardboard and a guy on a foldaway chair. Elation! The tramp turns out to be a lovely guy who got there at 4.30: undeniably impressive, we agree. None of us have queued for anything before, and we chat about the phone and our collective love for all things Apple. My initial elation, however, turns into uncertainty. Have we been duped by the pre-launch publicity? Have we horribly misjudged demand? By 6 a.m. a few more have joined, although we are still getting strange looks from the passers-by.

By 7.45, 15 minutes before the opening, there are about fifty people in the line, and those of us at the front are feeling pretty smug and pleased with ourselves. A guy arrives expecting, I think, to be one of the first people and is clearly disappointed. He trudges off to the back but five minutes later comes back up.

"OK, I'm going to put this out there. I'll buy your position off you."

Fantastic, this is what queuing is all about. What's he going to offer: £500? Or more? Perhaps four figures?

"£20. Cash."

I'm too stunned to say anything and so are the other two. This guy clearly hasn't a clue and definitely doesn't deserve the coveted pole position. He's rebuffed instantly and, despite an increase to £25, he has to retake his previous position.

When the doors open, there is a big cheer, and the three of us nervously walk in. Will the system crash? Will everything go through? Ten minutes later I am the first to walk out of the store with my brand new 3G iPhone.

I show it off like a trophy as I leave the store but then remember it's Nottingham I'm in and so quickly shove it into another bag and hurry to the car.

The cricket today was curtailed due to rain. Seeing the Surrey line-up has made me think about the parallels between us and the Surrey team of the 90s. They had four or five players in the England side who used to come in for the big one-day games. The announcement a few days ago of the provisional 30-man squad for the Champions Trophy contained five Notts players: Sidebottom, Broad, Swann, Pattinson and Patel. There is a decent chance that all five will make it into the main squad. It's great for all those involved and it reflects well on the club, but it does pose a challenge to have a strong enough squad to cover their absences.

As we were walking off for lunch I told Mark about my morning. I think he was impressed, even if he struggled to understand the extent of my enthusiasm for a phone. One of the things you can depend on is Mark's discretion, but I thought it prudent nonetheless to mention that it would be best if Mick didn't come to learn about my early morning escapade. "No problem, sweetheart." I felt a warm glow of appreciation.

This dissipated somewhat quickly when we stepped into the dressing rooms. "'Ere, Micky, you'll never guess where Waggy was this morning…"

Saturday 12 July

Trent Bridge, County Championship – Day Two
Surrey 356 for seven

Possibly the dullest day's cricket I've experienced. The weather was uninspiring: grey and mizzle most of the day. The run-rate only just made it over 2.5, thanks to some unorthodox hitting at the end of the day by Saqlain Mushtaq and some solid strokes from Chris Jordan who looks an excellent prospect. We could only gather a handful of wickets, all thanks to Darren Pattinson although Andre Adams bowled beautifully for no reward. Mark Ramprakash, who is on 99 first-class hundreds, looked as if he was going to bat for a week until Darren induced a leading edge. Overall, a day to forget.

Sunday 13 July

Trent Bridge, County Championship – Day Three
Surrey 403 all out (Pattinson 5-72)
Nottinghamshire 218 (Jefferson 42, Patel 40, Wagh 3) & 46 for two (Wagh 19)

Brittle batting has been a feature so far this season. Some rather injudicious shots (that's the most polite way I can describe some of the hacks) coupled with a couple of decent balls have put us in a precarious position. This evening, following on, I faced the best spell of bowling I've received this season. It came from 19-year-old Chris Jordan, the guy who impressed with the bat. He moved the ball through the air, off the pitch and all at a good lick. I loved the challenge, it really got the juices flowing. He could have nicked me off numerous times but I was pleased with the way I played; my balance was good and I held my shape well. I mentioned to Chris Read after the close how good I thought the spell was. He was surprised because he said from the changing rooms and on the video system, CricStat, it didn't look like it was doing much, which was slightly deflating to say the least. Graeme Swann says it's "like watching cricket on CCTV." I couldn't agree more. It also highlights how much of what happens in the middle is lost by the time it gets to the spectators, even if they are fellow players. I guess it's why I love playing so much more than watching. Those tussles between combatants which add sparkle and vim to the contest can only be appreciated by the players themselves sometimes.

I was absolutely devastated to get out in the fashion I did: caught down the legside off a Pedro Collins loosener. It was a particularly galling way to go, given the high quality of the battle to that point. Playing a bad shot or getting a good ball at least provides a definite conclusion, a victor and a vanquished. This dismissal offered neither, it was a misdirected ball and an acceptable shot. The bowler can't claim any credit, and I didn't play a poor shot. That's the second time I've been out like that this season, and everyone in the top five has been out in similar fashion. Mark Ealham said that, as a bowler, if you get one of those a season you've been lucky. I'm feeling pissed off, I think, because of the seeming lack of fairness about it: the contrast between that moment and what had happened in the 20 previous overs couldn't have been starker.

Monday 14 July

Trent Bridge, County Championship – Day Four
Surrey 403 all out (Pattinson 5-72)
Nottinghamshire 218 & 372 for six, declared (Patel 134*, Swann 68*, Adams 58)
Match drawn

Today was all about Samit's knock and what an innings it was. Mick had called for resolve and cool heads and Samit obliged with a superb century, ably supported by Graeme. He played with assurance and skill, knocking the ball to all parts of the ground. It was a fine demonstration of his talent, and a timely one given his inclusion in the provisional 30. It allowed us to claim the points for a draw which keeps us top of the table, if only by one point.

The team for tomorrow's Pro40 game against Worcester was announced after play. There's no place for Rob Ferley. He's very despondent this evening as he can't see a way into the side; he even thinks he won't make it into the T20 side if we play next week. He's performed well when he's had the opportunity, but unfortunately for Rob so has Samit. With Graeme back in the team, Mick evidently doesn't think he needs an extra spinner. Rob's girlfriend lives in Canterbury and he has a lot of friends in Kent and so these couple of years have been a bit of a sacrifice on the personal front. It's fortunate he has such an understanding girlfriend, but it's evidence of his desire to succeed in the game that he was willing to make such a move. So the disappointment of non-selection is compounded by the apparent pointlessness of the sacrifice.

Tuesday 15 July

Worcester, Pro40 League
Worcestershire 184 for nine
Nottinghamshire 188 for four (Shafayat 67*, Voges 64*, Wagh 7)
Nottinghamshire won by six wickets

A solid result gets our Pro40 campaign off to a good start. Kabir Ali bowled well at the start of our innings, but Adam and Bilal played excellently to ensure a comfortable win in the end. They both played with composure and skill, making the chase look easy when in fact the wicket had a little bit in it all the way through. I played poorly, feeling too tense and not patient enough: a throw back to the way I played one-dayers at Warwickshire. I need to do much better than this.

Last night, as a result of the appeal by Yorkshire, Glamorgan have taken our place in the quarter final. There was some disquiet within the team, as you would expect when a potential pot of gold has been taken away. My feelings, based on the not particularly popular view that going through was a most welcome but ultimately undeserved bonus, were neutral. I don't feel a sense of injustice like some of the guys, but I can certainly sympathise with those who do.

The season so far

County Championship – Division One

Canterbury	Kent	52		Won by 10 wickets
Headingley	Yorkshire	56		Drawn
Trent Bridge	Kent	42	21	Lost by 3 wickets
Trent Bridge	Lancashire	55	43*	Won by 7 wickets
Trent Bridge	Sussex	54	8	Lost by 73 runs
Old Trafford	Lancashire	94	0	Drawn
Southampton	Hampshire	66	67	Won by 6 wickets
Trent Bridge	Surrey	3	19	Drawn

M	Inn	NO	HS	Runs	Average	100s	50s
8	14	1	94	580	44.61	-	7

Table on 14 July

	P	W	L	D	Pts
Lancashire	8	3	1	4	97
Kent	8	3	2	3	96
Nottinghamshire	8	3	2	3	95
Durham	7	3	2	2	85
Yorkshire	8	2	3	3	85
Somerset	7	2	1	4	83
Surrey	8	-	2	6	73
Sussex	8	1	2	5	73
Hampshire	8	1	3	4	68

Friends Provident Trophy
Midland Group

Edgbaston	Warwickshire	-	Abandoned
Dublin	Ireland	0	Won by 56 runs
Trent Bridge	Northamptonshire	26	Won by 6 wickets
Trent Bridge	Leicestershire	37	Won by 2 wickets
Trent Bridge	Warwickshire	18	Lost by 52 runs
Northampton	Northamptonshire	-	Abandoned
Trent Bridge	Ireland	10	Won by 1 run
Oakham	Leicestershire	11	Lost by 13 runs

Quarter Final

Chester-le-Street	Durham	3	Lost by 1 wicket

M	Inn	NO	HS	Runs	Average	100s	50s
7	7	-	37	105	15.00	-	-

Pro-40 League – Division One

Worcester	Worcestershire	7	Won by 6 wickets

Chapter Nine

India

Whenever I visit Mumbai, I go through a similar process. First, I'm struck by the magnitude of the place, the throngs of people, the seeming chaotic road system, the dust, the refuse, the grime. But then I appreciate the vibrancy and the colours. I'm struck by the sheer effort people go to just to get food on the table. The juxtaposition of poverty and wealth is something that always takes my breath. It's a refresher for the mind. There couldn't be a greater contrast between orderly Britain and turbulent, messy, frantic India.

There is some irony that India is now completely revolutionising the cricketing landscape through the very medium it was initially reluctant to embrace: Twenty20 cricket. The emergence of the rebel ICL (Indian Cricket League) and the sanctioned IPL (Indian Premier League) has sent the various governing bodies scurrying for lawyers in a bid to secure the services of their own players in the face of a level of remuneration high enough to test the loyalty of even the most honourable of cricketers. Just where cricket is heading in the years to come is proving to be a fertile ground for discussion at the moment.

As I write this, the legal position between boards, players and the leagues is uncertain. It seems to me the ICC (International Cricket Conference), and the BCCI (Board of Control for Cricket in India) in particular, initially underestimated the potential revenues from a Twenty20 league, an error that was highlighted by the ICL. They realised that, without an officially sanctioned equivalent, they risked being sidelined, made irrelevant by their burgeoning rival. There isn't enough room in the international schedule to have two leagues whilst still having the stars representing their own countries, hence the stick and carrot approach: banning players from playing any other form of cricket if they play in the ICL, and the lure of huge salaries in the licensed league.

What impact will this have on English cricket? The most obvious scenario is that our best cricketers will be offered so much money that they decide that they can no longer refuse. Of course this isn't limited only to those centrally contracted players, but our best limited-overs players as well. When coupled with the renewed difficulty of acquiring a decent overseas player who is available for the majority of the season, this leaching of talent will lead to a lower standard of domestic cricket.

We were directly affected by the IPL when our overseas star, Dave Hussey, was 'bought' by Kolkata Knightriders, which meant he missed the start of the season for us. No one in the team begrudges Dave the chance to earn over a $1,000,000 primarily because we would have all done the same. This is the new environment in which county cricket is operating. Dimitri Mascarenhas missed the start of Hampshire's season for the same reason, and countless overseas player contracts have had to have been rewritten or ripped up.

Looking further ahead, I think the current salaries that are being offered will be dwarfed by huge sums in the years to come. India will be one of the biggest economies in the world in the next 15 to 20 years. Cricket is the only sport that matters to the population. Imagine the vast amount of money in all the American sports channelled into one. The other forms of the game will be under severe threat, especially if the IPL decide to play more series during the year.

The game is undergoing a seismic change: this is a revolution, not evolution. If Test cricket is to retain its stars, it makes sense to set aside a month each year for the competition. This allows players to make some money without compromising the standard of Test matches and without asking players to pit patriotism against pecuniary interests. I shall be interested to see whether the BCCI will share some of the spoils with the other governing bodies to compensate for any lost revenues from series that might have otherwise taken place. However it is accommodated, Twenty20 should be embraced and not feared. Change is inevitable, even in a venerable sport like cricket.

The PCA sent a text around the players asking whether we still viewed the Championship as the most important domestic competition. This was on the back of the (possibly premature) announcement of a Champions Trophy for the domestic winners from several countries and the Stanford games in the West Indies. The answer was yes, but whether this will remain the case is debatable.

Test cricket is only popular in a handful of the world's cricketing nations, and one-day 50-over cricket would appear to be a moribund form of the game. Twenty20 is the game's financial saviour; bringing opportunities to earn unheard of sums of money, ironically for the least amount of effort.

So let's imagine a cricketing landscape in 2020. County cricket in the UK revolves around a weekly game of Twenty20, with the best club teams playing in a Champions Trophy at the end of the summer. Test cricket is only played by amateurs from each country. The international teams play short series of Twenty20 against each other, culminating in a play-off at the end of the year between the top two for several million dollars each. Is this where cricket is heading?

Obviously I have no idea. There are however some important counter-arguments to the primarily financial thrust of Twenty20. Test cricket has been around for 135 years. It has heritage and prestige both amongst players and the public. Look at the Ashes 2005, a truly unique sporting event that captured the nation. Ask the current crop of players what they consider to be the pinnacle of cricketing achievement and, for most, Test cricket will be involved. Of course, this can change but for the moment the status of Test match cricket is very high. And to reiterate a point I made earlier in this diary, Twenty20 is relatively unproven. Domestically, counties are not selling tickets as easily as they once were, and indeed some are struggling to generate enough interest for all their games. And the ICC's broadcasting rights are underpinned by 50-over cricket until 2015. It may well be a little premature just yet to base the game's future around the most abbreviated form.

Given that 85% of domestic revenue comes from Test cricket, the four-day Championship still has a central role to play. It is certainly highly regarded by the players. The new regulations (96 overs/penalising slow over rate) have produced a competition that in my opinion is the best it has been: the shorter sessions have allowed captains to bowl their best bowlers for a greater proportion of the innings, thereby raising standards and ensuring each session is intensely competitive. Winning the Championship is an achievement of which to be immensely proud. It tests the resilience and skill of the individual, the ability of management to keep the ship on course and the resources and acumen of the club to build a squad strong and deep enough to cope.

However, the domestic structure will have to adapt to the new terrain. The financial imbalance between the forms of the game needs to be redressed: more money for winning Test matches internationally, and I'm delighted to see that the prize money for the Championship has increased substantially. Perhaps there are too many counties, some merging of the smaller ones may be necessary.

Twenty20 revenues are not cannibalising those from other forms yet. It is a wonderfully exciting, important part of the cricket offering. But it is only a part, not the whole.

Chapter Ten

Late July and August

Friday 18 July

Great news – Darren Pattinson is playing for England! It's come a bit out of the blue but, with an injury forcing Ryan Sidebottom out of the game, Darrren's got his chance. His bowling has been pivotal to us and, if he plays further Tests this summer, it will be a huge hole for us to fill. I have thought throughout the summer that he is international class, and I'm delighted that such a nice guy is getting a go.

His selection is causing a few grumbles on the grounds of his nationality and upbringing. Darren was born in Grimsby, emigrated to Australia when he was six and has held a British passport his whole life. I can see why people are complaining, simply because it seems hard to comprehend. What exactly does it mean to be British? Do you have to be brought up here? When does being 'brought up' end: five, ten, fifteen years of age? Is it about your passport? Your parents? It is a very emotive issue. I suspect it is very hard to generalise across cases: a set of circumstances which would make one person feel British might not have a similar effect on the next. Ten years in England might leave a permanent impression on one person but be forgotten after a couple of years in another.

It is a deep human instinct to seek similar people and view others less favourably. Families, tribes, gangs and of course religion are all based around commonalities which are viewed as good, whilst those that are different are considered bad. From the playground to politics and everything in between, group identity plays a prominent role. It offers a grounding in a seemingly chaotic world, a set of certainties which feed into our beliefs. It is no surprise, therefore, that, when an 'outsider' apparently is given membership of 'our' team, then emotions are likely to run strong.

In another development, the BCCI has prevented VVS Laxman from joining us for the last month of the season as we have players who have taken part in the unsanctioned ICL. This poses another headache for Mick as there is a dearth of quality players available due to the Champions Trophy.

I can't pretend that I'm not worried by these developments. Darren has taken 29 wickets including three five-wicket hauls this season. He has been the spearhead of out attack, someone to whom the captain has turned when we needed a breakthrough. And our batting has been vulnerable at times so, when Adam leaves in early August, we will need a class batter to fill his shoes. I'm sure Mick and Chris Read are scouring the list of available players. I suggested Stephen Fleming, but apparently he wasn't too keen. It will be interesting to see who we end up with.

There has also been the announcement regarding the creation of an English Premier League. A domestic Twenty20 will take the place of the Pro40 league. The idea of having all the centrally contracted players available, along with a host of overseas stars, certainly seems like it would appeal to the public. There are still some details to be resolved (like how many overseas players will be allowed and who the overseas teams will be) and the devil may well be hidden in them. We shall see.

I wonder if this is going to be too much though for the paying public. Will the subsequent Twenty20 competition, taking place without the stars during August and September, appear dull? Will they become desensitised to the format? These are certainly interesting times to be involved in the game.

Sunday 20 July

Trent Bridge, Pro40 League
Nottinghamshire 231 all out (Voges 85, Shafayat 45, Wagh 2)
Hampshire 200 for nine
Nottinghamshire won by 31 runs

The only thing that I will remember about this game is a throw. Penultimate over, Paul Franks has been hit for three sixes by Dimi Mascarenhas. Fifth ball is hit out to me at deep square leg. All I have to do is run in, pick it up and throw it to Chris in order to keep it down to a single and let Paul bowl at the number eleven. The first bit I did fine but, as I released the ball, I knew it was wrong and I saw it fly off to the right. It was horribly wide, and the batsmen trotted through for two. Paul decided to give me a volley of abuse, and I retreated to that place in my mind where that throw plays over and over. Where I can feel 8,000 sets of eyes all staring at me. Where all I want to do is replay the last minute as though it hasn't happened. I got called into the coach's office to have my fielding justifiably criticised. I can't describe how low I feel tonight. It seems that this season I've experienced greater low points than highs.

It's annoying because I feel like I'm moving quite well (I can just picture Chris and the others sniggering at that), and I've enjoyed fielding recently. Actually since Mick gave me a blast about my fielding a couple of months ago I've tried to improve, throw myself into every session.

I suppose it's just a case of riding out this low and getting back on the horse.

The game itself was a relatively straightforward victory after another excellent stand between Adam and Bil Shafayat. Billy got 45 and, between the two of them, got us to a challenging score. Andre Adams bowled beautifully and, with Charlie Shreck, took early wickets, putting the Hampshire Hawks behind the asking rate from the start. The two spinners,

Samit and Graeme, again bowled excellently through the middle, and we cantered home despite the late fireworks from Dimi.

I got a reasonable ball that came back in to trap me lbw. It started to swing just after I'd committed to playing the original line. But, as I write this, all I can think about is that throw. I'm off to bed and hope tomorrow is better than today.

Monday 21 July

Recovery this morning, followed by practice. Everyone was in, and Mick gave a half-way appraisal. He spoke about the good stuff (bowling, slip catching) and the areas we needed to improve on (scoring centuries). He also said that it would be a squad effort from now on, mentioning those out of the team at the minute who are waiting to play.

I did some work with Paul Johnson on the bowling machine again. I batted without my finger splint for the first time in a while. To be honest, my mind wasn't really on the job. The lows of this job seem to hit me harder than the highs, and I still felt a bit of a hangover from that throw yesterday. Slightly worryingly I felt terrible: arms, legs and body working independently with only a sparing thought about the ball. I've got a job to do tomorrow and have to put all these relatively inconsequential matters to one side and just bat – and bat well.

This afternoon we had our individual appraisals. These came into force three or four years ago when it became a legal requirement to give those in the last year of contract an idea of whether they would be offered a contract for the following year, but they are often extended to everyone, regardless of contractual position. Mick said I needed to score more one-day runs but that they wanted to extend my contract. Indeed, Mick said he wanted me to play here for the rest of my career.

It's pleasing that they are keen for this. I've been slightly worried about my future in the game, given the focus on Twenty20 cricket. I can't pretend that there aren't days when I wish I could do something else, as this diary tells. But I guess it's all I know at the moment, and I have no idea what I would do if I didn't play. And, as all the old timers say, you're a long time retired…

Tuesday 22 July

Trent Bridge, County Championship – Day One
Nottinghamshire 213 all out (Wood 58, Voges 45, Wagh 33)
Yorkshire 72 for five

The day started well. Paul apologised for his behaviour the other day. He was sincere and honest, and I really appreciated it. We won the toss and batted under a cloudy sky but with the promise of clear skies and sunshine. It was a borderline decision as the wicket had a tinge of green which added to the usual temptation to bowl first here at TB. Unfortunately the cloud remained for most of the day, and the ball nipped around. I loved the challenge of batting early on in testing conditions and was particularly pleased with the way things were going until I got one from Rana Naved that came back and clipped off stump. He is a wily bowler, always trying something, rarely bowling the same ball twice in a row. There were pockets of resistance with Matt Wood playing well for 58 and Adam Voges crafting a good 45. However, the ball was dominant today, and there was always a feeling that a wicket could come at any stage.

We bowled excellently, Charlie Shreck in particular. Graeme Swann took a great catch at second slip late in the day. I think it's going to be harder tomorrow if the sun is out. The mood in the camp was a little subdued at the turn around, but Chris emphasised that we could actually have a reasonable score, especially give the amount of deviation seen up to that point. There's a huge belief in the team about our bowling, not surprising when virtually every session we front up with the ball.

I've been really impressed with Andre Adams this summer. He is strong as an ox, trots in off a few paces, generates some decent pace and more often than not extracts movement from the wicket. As well as a dynamic fielder, he's a dangerous lower-order batsman. It's a bit of a surprise that he hasn't played more for New Zealand, something that I know he finds a little perplexing. He is also a gadget nut so there are always copies of the latest techo magazines lying around.

Our England contingent were on deck this morning. Ryan Sidebottom did some lung-busting fitness work before play, whilst Darren Pattinson and Stuart Broad popped in to say hello. Darren appeared a bit shell-shocked after the mauling he has taken from some quarters. The critics always say that they don't blame Darren himself, but that one line addendum at the end of an acerbic 500 words does little to emolliate the main thrust of the piece. We were all willing him to take a hatful of wickets and silence those critics. I just hope he hasn't gone to the back of the queue now.

Wednesday 23 July
Trent Bridge, County Championship – Day Two
Nottinghamshire 213 & 146 for two (Shafyat 62, Wagh 56*)
Yorkshire 161 all out (Shreck 5-58)

A very pleasing day. Charlie bowled beautifully this morning under a grey sky, swinging the ball both ways. We came a little unstuck when the last pair put on 56. We decided to give a single to Bresnan and try to bowl as many balls as possible at the number eleven, Kruis. However, by dropping all the fielders back, you lose a bit of intensity and, allied to Charlie coming off, the momentum shifted a little back to them. Fortunately it was restored first over after lunch when Mark Ealham trapped Bresnan lbw.

The Trent Bridge wicket, visited again by the pitch inspectors, seems to change depending on the overhead conditions. This morning the ball swung around in overcast conditions, but by the afternoon the cloud had burnt off, the sun was shining and it became a placid, benign surface. Billy and I put on just over a hundred. It was attritional stuff as they set relatively defensive fields and the ball seemed to go soft after about 30 overs. The balls this year have been poor, with umpires and players alike complaining about them going out of shape or losing hardness too frequently.

Billy played really well; he was a lot tighter in his defensive play than he was at the start of the year. He had just started to play some lovely shots when he was slightly unlucky to get caught off a deflection. Cricket is primarily an individual game but, when you are batting for a while with one person, it does become the two of you against the opposition, with each of you cajoling the other to greater efforts and to maintain concentration.

Again the battle against Rana Naved was the highlight for me. They were desperately trying to get the ball to reverse, throwing it into the square from the outfield and keeping the rough side as dry as possible. It didn't go as much as they would have hoped, but Rana still mixed up his action and the deliveries he bowled to make it hard work for us.

After the game, we invited the Yorkshire boys to the pub on the ground. It's a bit of a throw back to the old days, but it can only be a good thing to get to know the opposition a bit better – especially when Micky is buying the beers!

Thursday 24 July
Trent Bridge, County Championship – Day Three
Nottinghamshire 213 & 350 all out (Shafyat 62, Wagh 60, Patel 60, Swann 57)
Yorkshire 161 & 107 for four

This was a day of excellent cricket: solid batting and then consistent bowling. The key was Mark Ealham's spell with Chris up to the stumps. Having had little success bowling a channel outside off stump, he decided to attack the stumps. With his skiddy low action, he looked dangerous every ball.

Friday 25 July

Trent Bridge, County Championship – Day Four
Nottinghamshire 213 & 350
Yorkshire 161 & 290 all out (Ealham 7-59)
Nottinghamshire won by 112 runs

When I said earlier in the diary that four-day cricket is viewed as the best test of a team's capabilities, it was with games like this one in mind. The final result is a reflection of skill, perseverance and straightforward hard graft. For much of today it looked as though Yorkshire were going to pull off a seemingly unlikely victory with the ball not moving a jot and the wicket losing all pretence of menace. Adam Lyth made his maiden first-class century with worrying ease and, with the ball as soft as a sponge, wickets were scarce.

The outlook was grim, but up stepped Mark Ealham who, with Chris at the stumps, bowled a perfect spell of wicket-to-wicket bowling. Of the ten wickets he took in this game seven were lbw, two were caught behind or in the slips and one was bowled: testament to the impeccable line he bowled.

He took his 600th wicket during this game (prompting some wit to ask the veteran how many of them were still alive!). Mark hasn't exactly been under pressure this year, but I'm sure he will be relieved to have bagged some wickets.

Saturday 26 July

With yesterday's early finish and a BBQ at Graeme Swann's new house last night, it felt as if the weekend had started early. After a swim and a recuperative massage this morning, I had a great day strolling through West Bridgford. The sun was hot, and it felt like summer had finally arrived. And the beauty of it is that it's only Saturday!

I'm watching the final of the Twenty20 where it looks as if Middlesex are going to win. I don't think any of the pundits would have named Middlesex as winners before the start of the tournament (I'm not sure they themselves were that confident). But they came across a winning formula, in some ways helped by injuries which forced their hand. I think the lack of expectation might have initially helped them as they could play with the freedom that comes with underdog status until they had momentum and confidence in their abilities. To beat an excellent Kent team is deserving of acclaim, but to do so in a final is exceptional.

It is tempting to try to summarise some lessons gleaned from this year's competition:

Predicting a result is almost impossible.

The crucial battle is against the spinners through the middle of the innings.

The difference between any two teams is very small.

Find something that works and stick to it.

Fearlessness is crucial.

Sunday 27 July

The sports pages reporting on the final yesterday all focus on the money that is now available for the winners. This is in stark contrast to the rest of the paper, which is full of crunching credit. Perhaps in times of economic hardship, people are more highly tuned to the financial aspect of a story. I had lunch with a couple of the boys, and Charlie Shreck mentioned how a few years ago Tyrone Henderson playing for Kent tried to save a game against Notts by blasting the bowlers out of the park and failing, much to general amusement. It was with wry irony that he acknowledged that the boot is now firmly on the other foot.

One of the emerging aspects of Twenty20 cricket is the peripatetic nature of the cricketers involved who could simply travel between tournaments representing any team prepared to pay. Like travelling jugglers and acrobats of old, these modern-day entertainers dazzle the crowds with feats of extraordinary hitting and mesmerising bowling. It raises the question of what constitutes a team, stretching its identity. It's a little like the old spade handed down from great-great grandfather: it's just had a few changes of handles and heads. If you replace five of the regular team for the Twenty20 competition, is it still the same team? Will it evoke the same sense of loyalty from the fans?

Monday 28 July

Samit and I played in a benefit match for Jason Brown of Northamptonshire CCC this evening. It was thoroughly enjoyable and good fun to catch up with some of the other county cricketers there. It struck me how out of touch with the 'other' division cricketers are. Jimmy Anyon and Tony Frost, both at Warwickshire, were unsure how Division 1 was shaping up, and I was a little uncertain of the positions in Division 2.

Looking at the Division 1 table, it's clear that it is very tight with only 21 points separating top (us) from 6th (Sussex). Lancashire are 2nd, Durham and Somerset next (both with a game in hand), and Kent in 5th. With Durham twice and Somerset once in the next three weeks, the strength of our assault on the competition will be decided. The one crucial factor may well be that all our games at TB will be results, judging by recent history. So there will be plenty of points on offer; it's just a case of being on the right side. I guess we have to be fearless, not be concerned with failure. Which rather neatly brings me onto the subject of this week's game against Durham.

The pitch that has been requested is a used one that has been watered. The idea was to produce a benign spinning surface, although there is some concern that it may go up and down. So in trying to nullify the threat of their pace attack, we may have handed them a perfect surface for their tall, hit-the-wicket bowlers. Of course, we don't know how it will play out but I don't approve of the theory. We are a very good team, especially this week with Broad and Pattinson likely to be playing. By producing the wicket we have, we are sending out the signal that we are worried about the opposition. We should be preparing the best surface possible and back ourselves to be better than our opponents. After all, that's exactly what has got us to top of the league. It seems to me the equivalent of playing one way up to the final and then completely changing tactics. It also means that the toss is vital. We are putting all our chips on batting first and scoring big. I just hope the gamble doesn't back fire.

Tuesday 29 July

Charlie, Andre, Adam, Mark and I went to Birmingham to watch the latest Batman movie, *The Dark Knight*, at the Imax cinema. And what an experience it was. The quality of the picture was superb, and the scenes shot specifically for the huge Imax screen were breathtaking. Mark was comically grumpy, complaining about the journey, the queuing, the pick-and-mix selection, etc. But as soon as the first scene, a sweeping bird's eye view of the Gotham cityscape, took over the massive screen, he was hooked. Heath Ledger's valedictory performance was brilliant. Charlie, Andre and Adam are film aficionados, but we all agreed that it was one of the best films we'd seen.

I'm off to bed soon (just as soon as *Big Brother* finishes). I feel the usual anxieties on the eve of a game. I hope I sleep well tonight.

Wednesday 30 July

Trent Bridge, County Championship – Day One
Durham 266 all out (Shreck 4-69)
Nottinghamshire 6 for no wicket

What a great day! We bowled brilliantly and, even if I say so myself, I fielded really well. Let me do the bowling first. Yet again we excelled with the ball and dismissed a talented line-up cheaply (there is a caveat which I'll come to). Charlie Shreck was in the wickets, backed up with tight spin bowling from Samit and Graeme. But here's the caveat: too often a delivery kept low, and the wicket looks like it is deteriorating. So what is a below-par score on a good wicket, which for the majority of today it was, may well be an average-to-good score on tomorrow's. I'm really angry about the pitch. Why couldn't we just play them on a good surface? All our wickets today came from good bowling: we don't need to doctor. In doing so, we may have shot ourselves in the foot.

On to fielding. Too often in this diary I have had to relate a fielding error and the morale sapping effect it has had on me. Well, today my fielding made me feel a million dollars. A little technical tip from Adam during practice yesterday seems to have helped me enormously. There were no great catches, just solid ground fielding and every time I dived for a ball I stopped it. I felt fantastic. There is always the worry at the back of my mind that a cock up is just round the corner, as two steps forward, one step back has been the story of my fielding this year so far. But today was one-way progress and, whatever happens next time, I can look back at today's efforts with pride.

Thursday 31 July

Trent Bridge, County Championship – Day Two
Durham 266
Nottinghamshire 114 for four (Shafayat 54*, Wagh 2)

A frustrating day for spectators and players alike as rain and bad light reduced play to 30 overs. Billy played really well, and Samit was looking in excellent form until he clipped one to mid-wicket. I got what I thought was a reasonable ball from Harmison which just bounced a little, forcing an edge to slip. Mick had a different view: he thought it was a 'soft dismissal'. Well, it wouldn't be a day at the ground unless he had a pop at me, I guess! I thought I did fine, but perhaps his prompting will push me onto greater efforts. I spoke to Steve Harmison about the ball, and he agreed with me. I might mention it if I catch Mick in a good mood in the morning.

The pitch itself has mercifully played well. We have had to battle with humid, swinging conditions; it's tough when the clouds cover TB. We now need to bat most of tomorrow and put them under pressure on the last day. Of course, batting for a whole day here is a tall order so it's more likely to be a scrap with a nervy run chase at the end.

This evening AJ Harris had a darts event as part of his benefit year. A few of the Durham guys were there, and we played a version of cricket darts – a slightly uneasy amalgam of the two sports but one which provided much amusement. The standard was abysmally low, and at one point I thought we were never going to get the ten 'wickets' (don't ask!) we needed. After about an hour of toil, thankfully we cobbled together enough reasonably successful throws to finish the game. I think everyone was relieved, none more so than the bar manager who must have wondered if he would need to extend his licensing hours!

Darren Pattinson has landed himself in hot water after some comments he made to an Australian radio station were picked up by the local media. They implied that he would rather spend his winter in Australia than play for England. In fact, he was asked what he thought he was most likely to do this winter, and he replied honestly that he didn't think England would select him. This was twisted to suggest a desire which didn't exist. I chatted to him a bit today, and it's clear that he has been thrown into a situation he is still coming to terms with. When he signed for us this year, he expected to be here for half the year and in Melbourne for the rest. Now his rapid rise has thrown all his plans into confusion. His main concern is for his young family and providing for them on the one hand but also being there for them on the other. It's a not uncommon situation for a sportsman, and there are no easy solutions. He has a contract with Cricket Victoria, which he has to weigh up against the chances of playing for England. He is wary of the 'one-Test wonder' scenario and doesn't want to throw away a good contract for nothing. If he gets selected on an England A tour, he has to decide whether it is worth the gamble to ditch Victoria. A simple question for a young guy with no commitments, but a different kettle of fish for a father of two.

I chatted to him during the day and simply said what I imagine a lot of people are thinking. He has been the stand-out bowler this year in county cricket, and it would be a shame if someone with so much talent didn't get the chance to express it at the highest level. It would also make a mockery of any selectoral claims for consistency if he went from next-in-line to out-of-the picture after one performance. And, of course, two or three years of international cricket would be very nice for the bank balance, thank you very much.

Friday 1 August
Trent Bridge, County Championship – Day Three
Durham 266 & 72 for two
Nottinghamshire 268 all out (Shafayat 100)

In many ways Billy is well ahead of his 24 years. He made his debut as a 16-year old, with the attendant notes of exciting potential and promise. Events rarely pan out in the expected fashion, and a spell at Northamptonshire was required when he fell out of favour at Nottingham. It's probably been fair to say that his return has been a little low key up to now. There have been signs over the last few weeks, however, that he is in good nick and this hundred was one of the best. He scored 100 out of 177 with a mixture of steely broad-batted defence and wristy flicks through the leg side. There was a calm assurance about his innings, something that I've alluded to previously. And yesterday's runs came in perfect bowling conditions against a high quality attack. I'm sure he will take a great deal from this knock. How much of an effect one innings can have on a career is questionable, but certainly in the short term it should be a huge reinforcement of his approach as well as confirming to both himself and others that he is indeed an opening batsman.

The Durham reply was characterised by defence: 72 runs coming off 47 overs with Chanderpaul scoring seven off 75 balls. The wicket is basically dead, once the new ball has passed, and there is some turn out of the rough. But it's not a minefield, and it seems that Durham are happy to take a draw. I'm not saying we wouldn't do the same if we found ourselves in the same situation – who knows? – but the bottom line is that it was exceptionally dull cricket to watch. Some spectators booed the batters as they left the ground. It disappoints me because four-day cricket can be so good, but this is just going to drive people away from the format. I think there is some onus on the teams to play positive cricket, to provide some entertainment. If you then find yourself in trouble, the subsequent effort to recover is just as captivating to watch as a run chase. It was basically a one-innings shoot out with 143 overs left: surely enough time for a game? No doubt the Durham view is very different; I'm just frustrated for both us and the spectators.

Rob Ferley has had an interesting week as captain of the second team. He called one of the trialists by the wrong name for three days, had another one refuse to move when fielding because he wasn't being bowled and, despite "bowling my little heart out" from one end, he received a reprimand from Wayne Noon for not bowling anyone else. Rob's deadpan narration of events was most amusing although I think he may have been looking for a more sympathetic reaction from his landlord.

Saturday 2 August
Trent Bridge, County Championship – Day Four
Durham 266 all out & 257 for eight (Broad 4-39)
Nottinghamshire 268
Match drawn

Was it our own fault for producing this wicket? In the end, it didn't disintegrate but it was lifeless. Durham, with their game in hand over us, were happy to play out for the draw. It was boring to play in and to watch. I've already stated my opposition to the thinking behind the choice of wicket. The fact that the spinners who were supposed to bowl us to victory only took two wickets between them in the game shows that trying to load the dice in our favour doesn't work (I'm discounting Adam's three wickets as the game was already over by then). I felt that given a normal surface our seamers could have won us the game in the crucial third innings, but they weren't given a chance on this wicket. If we had a game in hand on Durham, then I could just about support the decision, but we don't and a win against these guys could have been huge.

Through the despondency that the two-runs-per-over rate produced, there was a ray of sunshine. Stuart Broad bowled straight with a hint of swing to claim four for 39. I'm sure there is always a desire to show the selectors what they are missing when an international player gets dropped. He seemed to accept his lot with magnanimity. England lost the Test match at Edgbaston today and with it the series so perhaps a period out of the firing line isn't the worst thing.

I'm currently in the car with Rob Ferley. He has been selected in the squad for tomorrow's Pro40 game against Gloucestershire. I think it's elevated his spirits although I can't be sure. He is plugged in to his iPod, listening to a selection of poker podcasts and is therefore uncommunicative. It would be a little surprising to play three spinners tomorrow but, if we do, at least we'll get through our overs quickly! The Cheltenham College pitch has been a haven for batters this week; Matt Wood says it's a very small ground. I just hope I can get in and help us win. I feel a bit under pressure in the one-dayers as I haven't nailed a score yet. Last year, when I did well, I had a very similar mentality to that in Championship cricket, with the addition of the odd premeditated shot when required. Tomorrow I'm going to focus on the battle with each bowler rather than worry too much about the scoreboard. Let's see what happens.

Looking ahead over these next couple of weeks, we have Somerset and Durham again, both away. I much prefer the comforts of home and so I'm not too thrilled at the prospect of two weeks in hotel rooms and car seats. When I first started, I loved it. What with going for dinner each night and staying in plush hotels, it felt like a mini-holiday. Now the appeal has waned somewhat although, if you play well, then it's particularly enjoyable to be surrounded by team mates in the evening.

Sunday 3 August

Cheltenham, Pro40 League
Nottinghamshire 208 for eight (Patel 65, Wagh 28)
Gloucestershire 92 for four (19 overs)
Nottinghamshire won by 9 runs (by Duckworth-Lewis)

I was checking the radar during the day, and it was pretty clear that we were in line for a lot of rain; the only question was when would it arrive.

In the end, we couldn't have been more fortunate. Gloucester were well ahead of the Duckworth-Lewis throughout their innings until a brilliant three-wicket burst from Mark Ealham put us ahead just as the rain came in. My favourite wicket of the three was Alex Gidman. Paul Franks must have said "Keep it off his pads" at least five times in the break between wickets as Alex came to the crease. So when he was out second ball, leg before wicket, there was a fair degree of micky taking. One of the guys described this win as a 'burgle', and that about sums it up. I think if the game had run its course we probably would have won, but we'll never know and the bottom line is that the only time we were ahead was at the end.

We won the toss and batted on what everyone expected would be a road. Unfortunately it was anything but, with the ball deviating off the seam at pace. I played well until I played one off my legs, only to see Steve Kirby diving to his left and taking an excellent catch at short fine leg. I was obviously disappointed as I felt I had seen off the best of their attack. I was focussing on trying to move as late as possible and trusting myself that I would have time to react. I think it worked well, and it's something I will have to remember this week.

Samit again played well. He is having an excellent season, contributing with both bat and ball. I will be interested to see if he gets picked for higher honours in the coming month. Today it was announced that both Michael Vaughan and Paul Collingwood have resigned their captaincies. With a new captain, rumoured to be Kevin Pietersen, I'm sure there will be a new look team. If Samit is part of that he can be assured of a decent run, I would have thought.

There is a parallel at this stage of the season with last year: top of both the Championship and the Pro40. We finished second in both last year – are there any lessons we can learn? We were on the wrong end of a ferocious injury list in 2007, and I think we are a stronger squad this year. We are in a position at the moment where we can rest a bowler for a game and have them coming back strong in the next. So we should have the personnel to prevent a slide like last year. Then there are all the clichés: remain focused, concentrate on what we do best, control the controllables, et al.

Tuesday 5 August

Samit has been picked in the England one-day squad, along with Ryan, Stuart, and Graeme; Darren is in the England Lions team. It's great news but stretches us to the absolute limit. Matt Wood and I have been talking about our final two months and how we are shaping up. Losing both Samit and Graeme is going to be a real test, especially in the Pro40 where they are integral with both bat and ball. We can't afford any injuries or loss of form. It makes our challenge for honours look difficult to say the least. A silver lining is that Rob should figure in all the rest of the games (at least bowling his heart out last week has been worth it!). Will Jefferson will also return on the back of some decent form in the second team.

In addition we have three guys in the England under-19s, which means we have eight players involved in the national set-up; impressive but also a bit of a headache. I've already mentioned the similarity between us and Surrey of the 90s (although I could have cited Lancashire or Yorkshire who have also provided a large number of England players). The importance of having a squad strong enough to cover for the absentees but equally having the cohesion and understanding to cope when they return is crucial. There's also the difficulty that can arise from putting out two different teams. Just as imperative is integrating the internationals when they come back. These are issues Mick will be grappling with: he will certainly be tested in the weeks to come.

I'm writing in the passenger seat again, this time with Matt driving us to Taunton. I'm not feeling too swish having overindulged slightly last night. Jamil and his fiancée Tammy came up. We were joined by Gary Speed, the footballer. It turns out Gary is an ardent cricket fan so I tried to get him to come to one of our games and play in our warm-up football. Unsurprisingly he wasn't too enamoured with the suggestion despite my telling him we play a no-tackling rule so he shouldn't get hacked down.

The weather is awful (summer? really?), and the forecast isn't great for tomorrow, Thursday or Saturday. Somerset are another team that have a game in hand on us, but I can't see them playing as defensively as Durham did. The fact that they are at home and they soundly beat us last year in the corresponding fixture means they should be confident.

Matt is returning to his old club for the first time. He's a bit nervous, as I guess anyone would be. He's keen for us to show his old team how good we are, which is exactly how I felt when we played Warwickshire last year. I really hope that he gets some runs, not only from the team perspective but because I know how much they will mean to him.

Wednesday 6 August
Taunton, County Championship – Day One
Somerset 106 all out (Pattinson 5-40)
Nottinghamshire 185 for six (Patel 56, Wagh 46)

A straw-coloured, easy-paced pitch full of runs: that is the usual expectation when you play a game at Taunton. So, when we turned up this morning and had to have the wicket pointed out to us, indistinguishable as it

was from the rest of the green square, it's fair to say there was some disappointment amongst the batters. It looked almost like a park wicket: patchy green tufts of grass, soft underfoot, and dark, wet soil beneath. Apparently, they took an inch of top soil off the square over the winter, and they have struggled to get the grass to grow ever since.

Mercifully we won the toss. The ball seamed and swung all morning and we bowled them out just after lunch. Darren did his usual stuff and took another five wickets. There were muted celebrations after each wicket, though, from the batting contingent as we realised that we would soon be on the receiving end.

When Matt Wood nicked off in the first over, I was fearing the worst as I walked out. But I saw the first ball reasonably well and settled in ok. I was a bit anxious to get off the mark, haunted as ever by the spectre of 'baggage' – ducks in both innings. When I knocked one down to fine leg, I trotted up, a relieved man, to the other end.

I was playing well and then clipped a ball uppishly to square leg and was caught (familiar story?). 'Frustrated' doesn't even touch the way I felt as I walked off. I wanted to wrap my bat around something, just scream and let it all out. I can't tell you why I hit it in the air; can I put it down to 'one of those things'? I generally shy away from too much analysis of my batting, being a strong believer in the 'paralysis through analysis' school. But part of me is starting to think I should do something to start converting these starts into substantial contributions. I suppose in the context of the game it's a valuable effort, but I should have posted a match-winning effort from the position I was in.

Playing against Justin Langer there were times during the day when I wondered what he thought of me, if anything. He has a reputation of not suffering fools gladly, being a hard, uncompromising man. Of course, any opinion of me would be based on inference as I don't think I've ever actually spoken to him – he just glowers at me when on the pitch.

I had dinner this evening with Ealy, Mick and Billy. Mark was not impressed with his seemingly new role in the team: change-of-ends bowler. He even had to bowl that over from his least preferred end! There was a reasonable degree of leg-pulling during the day, especially from Paul Franks. Mark obviously took it well (he dishes out more than his fair share), and his slightly peeved air this evening was very funny.

Thursday 7 August

Taunton, County Championship – Day Two
Somerset 106 & 114 for no wicket
Nottinghamshire 230 all out (Read 74*)

This was easily our worst day for a long while. We lost our four overnight wickets too cheaply this morning. Then Langer and Trescothick took the attack to us, and we had no answer.

The mood in the dressing room was sombre during the first hour. We wanted to retain the momentum from the previous day and lock Somerset out of the game. Instead, as batsman followed batsman, we were squandering a potentially match-winning position. Chris played really well with the tail, hitting boundaries and manipulating the strike. But, when we lost our final wicket, no one wanted to catch Mick's eye as he was incensed with our performance.

Nevertheless, we had a lead of over 120 on a seaming, swinging wicket. All we needed were two big wickets at the top of the order, and we felt we could get into the rest of their batting. Backed into a corner, Langer and Trescothick came out fighting. It was Langer initially who took the attack to us, cutting and driving his way to a belligerent 50. He could have been run out twice, so keen was he to dominate in everything he did. And how different the day could have been if the throws had hit.

Instead, our lead wasn't chipped away, it was blown to smithereens. Taking the lead from his partner, Trescothick started to drive crisply down the ground and pulled anything short. As when two batters get in, the wicket looked flat. Bereft of the potency that had been so prevalent in our bowling attack up to that point, we floundered trying to stem the flow of runs.

The saving grace was that it rained, keeping the day short. It gives us a chance to regroup and forces them to start again. This game is now completely open. We don't want to chase more than 250, as there are always a few nerves when it comes to our batting. I thought Alfonso Thomas bowled well for them, moving the ball around at decent pace, and Charl Willoughby was his usual dependable self. A win would be huge for us, in terms of both points and the huge confidence boost we would have. We need a win also because we are losing some key members over the next few weeks.

So when Chris took one on the thumb and had to go to hospital to have it checked out, I'm sure everyone else was wondering whether this would be another debilitating blow. Fortunately it looks as if it was just dislocated, and he is hopeful of playing tomorrow. We're going to need a bit of luck in the run-in, as any potential champions do. Often it is bare-faced chance that separates equally deserving teams: nothing more, nothing less.

I'm interested to see what condition the ground is in tomorrow morning. We had a lot of rain this afternoon and, when I left, there were sizeable puddles covering large swathes of the outfield and square.

Friday 8 August
Taunton, County Championship – Day Three
Somerset 106 & 335 all out
Nottinghamshire 230 & 63 for three (Wagh 13)

This was a hard-working day. We battled to get the breakthrough in the morning. It came courtesy of Charlie Shreck who induced Langer to guide one to slip. Trescothick went next, caught in the gully off Andre. There followed a procession of 20s, as we worked our way through the rest of their batters. The ball did less than on the first day, just a hint of swing and seam. Even the tail-enders played with relative ease, something that's always frustrating, but at least it showed that the pitch held few demons.

I couldn't stop thinking about how different things would have been if either of the two throws had run Langer out early yesterday. But I suppose that's cricket, and it's not often 'what might have beens' play a significant part in proceedings.

We have a really good bowling unit, complementing one another perfectly. With Charlie's swing, Darren's pace, Andre's guile, Mark's accuracy and our twirling spinners we test the abilities of every batter. There have only been two hundreds scored against us this year, a reflection of both conditions and personnel.

My feeling is that average scores around the country are much lower than usual. Two-hour sessions, 96-over days and regular rain fall have combined to make it a tough summer for batsmen. A total of over 400 draws attention at the moment, not the usual state of affairs. Mick has mentioned several times this year that in these low-scoring games it's vital we win as we aren't picking up bonus points. In previous years, solid draws with maximum bonus points would be sufficient to ensure at least mid-table solidity. It makes for exciting cricket, though, (last week excepted) and high blood pressure for Mick.

Chasing 212 to win, we have lost three wickets: Billy, Matt and me. It would be a nervy run chase except for the weather: it is supposed to rain all day tomorrow. A win would obviously be priceless and put us back on top of the table. I think we need at least 35 overs to score these runs and, if the apocalyptic forecast is correct, there is very little chance of that.

111

I'm sure Somerset would be keen to play as well, fancying their bowlers to knock us over.

Chris's thumb is still stiff and sore despite receiving treatment on the hour every hour. I think it's touch and go whether he plays on Sunday. Will Jefferson is on standby, should the injured digit not recover in time. Chris has been wandering around with his thumb in a glass of either ice-cold or hot water and, when not immersed, holding it aloft above his head to try to get the swelling down. For a leader by example it must be torture to watch from the sidelines, although he seems to be pretty relaxed at the moment.

Saturday 9 August
Taunton, County Championship – Day Four
Somerset 106 & 335
Nottinghamshire 230 & 125 for four (Patel 42*)
Match drawn

The rain had the last say. Samit was playing well and Andre had struck a few violent blows, but once the rain started that was that. Everyone was lamenting the weather; everyone realised how valuable this win could be. Adam was positive about the situation, noting that we are 11 points further on and at least the ball is in our court. At the head of the table we have to play good cricket and let the others worry.

It was a tedious, repetitive day. As the rain eased off, the radar was checked, hopes were raised slightly and then it would rain again. The covers ebbed and flowed, the groundsmen cursing the weather as much as we did. I had a couple of nets with Mick on the bowling machine after the newspapers were exhausted and I had finished reading my book (*A Fine Balance* by Rohinton Mistry, one of the best I've read).

I tried to pen a few words for Jamil and Tammy's wedding (now happening next week). I struggled to get much down; the Taunton dressing rooms didn't offer much inspiration.

I feel a bit flat this evening. I'm putting it down to a lack of runs. I didn't fancy going out for dinner with the guys and have just eaten in my room. Sometimes I just feel a little low and need 24 hours to get back to normal. I also need to get some thoughts down for a speech I'm doing in a couple of weeks' time at the under-14 festival where an England Schools team is picked. The organiser, Hugh Cherry, is a lovely man, and I've known him for donkey's years. I'm quite looking forward to it, as long as I can think of some good material. Hugh suggested I address it primarily at the boys: offer advice, reminisce a little, that sort of thing.

Sunday 10 August

Taunton, Pro40 League
Nottinghamshire 240 for seven (Voges 68*, Jefferson 53, Wagh 34)
Somerset 241 for seven (39.5 overs, Swann 4-35)
Somerset won by three wickets

The crowd enjoyed it at least. A game in which we were ahead for large swathes was eventually decided by two innings, one of 22 balls and one of 23. The two batters were James Hildreth (38) and Wes Durston (36) respectively.

Mark Ealham, captain for the day as Chris's thumb hadn't recovered, won the toss and batted. We started well: Will and I played nicely on an ugly looking, but easy-paced, wicket. Adam kept the momentum going nicely in the middle. When it looked like we were losing our way towards the death, Paul Franks biffed the final over for 24. We were happy with our total of 240, knowing that we needed two big wickets at the start and then our spinners could do what they've done all season.

Charlie Shreck snared Justin Langer for the third time in the week, caught behind in the first over. There followed a decent stand between Trescothick and Kieswetter of 73 but, when Graeme bowled Marcus with a beauty, I thought we had done it. They needed 144 off 24 overs.

The required rate climbed, hitting 9.5 runs per over, and showed no signs of slowing. Enter James Hildreth. He struck the ball beautifully, injecting hope into the Somerset chase. From looking like a lost cause, suddenly it was all up for grabs again. Just when it looked like the game could be going away from us, Graeme came back on and dismissed Hildreth. Swanny varied his pace and spun the ball hard. He was a class act, and his final figures of four for 35 off eight overs were richly deserved. We were back in it.

But then there was a ball change. The umpires can change the ball if it gets scuffed and therefore becomes difficult to pick up. The problem with this is that our ball was relatively soft and difficult to hit; the replacement, in contrast, was rock hard. I can understand the need for visibility, but the difference in hardness changed the course of the game.

Wes Durston took full advantage of the new ball, carrying on from where Hildreth had left off. Taunton is such a small ground straight towards the old pavilion, it's almost impossible to defend if someone strikes the ball cleanly. And Wes certainly did that. He hit sixes over long-on and long-off. We didn't really have an answer and when he was out, they only needed a run a ball which at Taunton isn't a contest.

So, driving back up the M5, both Matt and I feel like we've lost two games. It was Chris Read's 30th birthday today, not a particularly happy day. Mark Ealham was introspective as I left the ground, wondering if there was anything he could have done differently as captain. Ultimately it was two innings that he could do little about that were the pivotal points of this game.

Mick pointed out in his summation at the end of the game that that was our first loss for six weeks. We have been playing some excellent cricket. He said that every game is important from now on in and that we need to focus on this week's challenge against Durham, which is an especially important game.

I'm fortunate that I'm playing for a club that is in the hunt for two trophies. In the old days, before two divisions, there must have been so many dead games at this time of year. The tension in the middle was fantastic: it shows how much this game meant to everyone. I was nervous scouting round the boundary, worried about messing up in such tight conditions but nevertheless wanting the ball to come my way as a piece of good fielding was so valuable.

I'll sleep well tonight after the stress of the day. It seems to have happened so quickly, but we are coming towards the end of the season. The success or failure of our efforts will be measured by the outcome of the next few weeks.

Monday 11 August

My neck is a little sore as I write this. I was doing a pull up this morning in the gym when I heard a crunch and my upper back and neck went into spasm. It's eased up a lot since then, and I'm fairly sure I'll be fine for tomorrow's game against Durham. It's been a nuisance, though, on this our only day off in two weeks.

Mick described this as a "can't lose" game. With the usual forecast for rain, it wouldn't surprise me if there was no result. The only counter-argument is that the wicket might be lively, to say the least. Last week's pitch against Kent at the Riverside caught the attention of the inspectors and the ire of Kent captain Rob Key. Let's see what they produce this time.

I've been trying to catch up with laundry, post, house work and bills today. I've also tried to get my gear sorted out for Jamil and Tammy's wedding this weekend. I would say I've accomplished about 3%. Some kind of time management course for me this winter, I think.

One aspect of last week that has made a real impression on me is Marcus Trescothick's batting. I fielded square of the wicket to him for a while, and it allowed me to appreciate his footwork and balance. I had the mistaken impression from the TV that he didn't move his feet much, whereas in fact he does use the crease well and he always plays the ball under his eyes. He must have a selection of great bats as well as superb timing, because some of his little pushes raced off towards the boundary.

I particularly enjoyed the seeming simplicity of his technique. As with all skilled artisans, his performance looked effortless. I would love to take that facet of his game and add it to mine. At Worcester a few weeks back, we were compiling lists of top threes. Marcus appeared in best player of fast bowling, best player of spin bowling and best slip fielder. He is an enormously talented player and a huge loss to England.

Tuesday 12 August
Chester-le-Street, County Championship – Day One
No play – rain

We had started warm-ups at 10 a.m. when it started drizzling. From then until the early hours we experienced the full spectrum of rainfall from heavy to light.

Fortunately we are staying in a good hotel just next to the Metro Centre so it was shopping and coffee this afternoon, something I think may be repeated again this trip.

Friday 15 August
Chester-le-Street, County Championship – Day Four
Match abandoned, no play

I can't believe it's only been four days. It's felt like we've been in Durham a month at least. It has rained almost continuously since Tuesday. The sunshine today came too late as the outfield resembled a marsh. A silver lining was that the umpires were sensible and called the game off first thing, which at least meant we could head home and miss the traffic. I don't think I've ever played in a championship game with not a ball bowled. With all the equipment at grounds these days it doesn't take long to clear any water. The fact that we didn't even get close to playing shows how much rain has fallen.

The hotel-shopping-centre circuit was run ad nauseam, not bad for fitness actually as I must have walked about three miles each trip.

Mick had a couple of minutes just before we headed off. He said he didn't want us going flat after this week and only one game in the next two weeks. It's been a funny season for scheduling: it seems as though we have either been playing non stop or had nothing to do for days. It will give everyone the chance to get their thoughts together for the 'final push'. The bowlers in particular will need to start calling on those reserves of energy as there will be no rest for our main players.

We said goodbye to Adam Voges; he's heading back to Australia for a pre-season camp with the Australian squad. I've enjoyed watching him bat, and he has been really helpful with my fielding. He probably hasn't scored as many championship runs as he would have liked, but he has been our most consistent one-day batter, and his own fielding has been brilliant. He bats with a rare elegance but is almost violent when he goes for a cover drive or cut. I hope he comes back next year but, with either international commitments or an IPL contract in the offing, I think it's unlikely.

He's been a real hit in the changing room. He's taken all the cracks about being the whitest Australian ever with good humour and gives as good as he gets.

I'm off to Jamil's wedding this weekend in posh Portofino. The Rooneys got married in the same place apparently. I seem to have packed enough for a fortnight, not the two nights I'll be there. Jamil has texted, saying that the local dress code seems to be 1950s Italian Riviera: lots of crisp white shirts and cigarette holders. Given that my wardrobe is more Birmingham 1990s, I could stand out somewhat.

Monday 18 August

It was with disbelief I flew back this morning. The post-holiday downer kicked in as soon as we came through the low, grey cloud base and it started raining. I could only chuckle when a girl, on the phone to a friend of hers, declared in a wonderful Essex accent, "I've only been back three seconds and I f***ing hate it already."

I'm going to find it difficult to describe the weekend and sufficiently convey the sense of the extraordinary. The most important fact was that it was a quite brilliant wedding. Jamil and Tammy were ecstatically happy; the small but perfectly formed wedding party were great company, and I had a ball. It started when I stepped off the plane. Coming from the week of rain we've just had to beautiful warm sunshine instantly perked me up. Then driving my little hire car to Portofino along the winding coastal road was great fun. I lost count of the number of times I had to shut my eyes as scooters or pedestrians narrowly escaped with their lives as I horribly misjudged the near side from the wrong side of the car.

And then the venue. Hotel Splendido, a former monastery, and now so aptly named, is a luxury retreat of epic proportions. George Clooney, Elton John, Richard Branson and Gary Linekar had only recently checked out, and we were treated like royalty. Nothing was too much trouble. It was a place where the guests rarely worried about such trivialities as cost (prices were notably absent from the menus). To be honest, the slightly fawning service wasn't exactly to my taste, but I quickly overcame any grumbles and adapted to my new-found status as a superior being for whom only the best was good enough.

We drank vintage champagne, the finest of wines and the freshest of seafood. It was a truly divine weekend. I thought it was going to be good, but I hadn't expected it to be this amazing.

At least now I know what my life will be like when I win the lottery. With a huge rollover, I think I could probably afford at least one long weekend a year at the Splendido.

I drove straight back to Trent Bridge for a practice under the floodlights. I met our new overseas player, Ashwell Prince, the South African vice-captain. He looked confident and very approachable. It's been a difficult task to find a player of sufficient quality to fill Adam's boots but, from first impressions, Mick has done a fine job.

It was a comedic session. I had possibly the worst net any professional has ever had, barely able to lay a bat on anything, and when I did all I could manage was a nick to the keeper. But then the real fun started with fielding practice. Normally under a skier, by the time the ball has reached its zenith, the fielder knows approximately where the ball will land. However, when the ball left the bubble of light over the ground, it was impossible to see and hence when the ball began dropping you could find yourself nowhere near it, necessitating some last-minute scrambling. There were some classic moments with the fielder – hands aloft, eyes lifted skywards – watching the ball land several metres away.

Tomorrow's game is on Sky so any cock-ups will be replayed for all to see. Rob "I never drop catches in practice" Ferley couldn't lay a hand on his skiers, leaving us all chuckling and Mick in his trademark tea-pot stance.

Tuesday 19 August

Trent Bridge, Pro40 League
Durham 178 for nine
Nottinghamshire 146 for nine (25 overs, Wagh 50 ret hurt, Jefferson 43)
Durham won by 6 runs (by Duckworth-Lewis)

I woke with my usual feeling of dread: all the scenarios of me failing flood through my mind in that first waking moment. But once up and in the shower I manage to convince myself that maybe today won't be as bad as I expect. It's a funny routine and one that in many ways is motivating: I always understand when a sportsman says he is driven by a fear of failure. It takes courage to put yourself in a position where you can fail, and to do so repeatedly requires a method to cope and indeed thrive.

For me, I try to identify precisely what it is I'm worried about, rationally evaluate the chances of it happening and then imagine myself doing well in that situation. It only takes a few moments, but I think you need to be honest with yourself at this point because otherwise you're not addressing the actual concern.

During warm-ups a huge black cloud covered the ground and made it feel like the depths of winter. Durham, because the rain had prevented them practising for a week, decided to start early and practically had had a training session before we had even got onto the field.

I struck the ball well in the pre-match throw downs, sometimes a good sign sometimes not. I had Kevin Paxton, the fitness trainer, throwing his usual erratic assortment. I much prefer having him, though, because I don't need someone thinking about my technique in the minutes before the game. And, of course, he makes me laugh.

We lost the toss and fielded. I walked out with Ealy, who was slightly concerned about his return to the slip cordon, as the last time he was in the slips on TV he dropped a straightforward chance. Sometimes I don't know how he gets himself onto the field, he's always so pessimistic about his chances and convinced his body is about to give up the ghost. Certainly makes me chuckle though.

We got off to a bad start; at one stage the projected score showed 360 at the current rate. Chanderpaul and Mustard played well – but worryingly, despite their scoring, when we hit just back of a length the ball looked unplayable. Of course, this is just the length that Harmison would be hitting later (and under lights as well).

Rob Ferley turned it round for us with two wickets that slowed Durham down and brought us back into the game. He got the vital wicket of Benkenstein, caught cover, and from then on we were in control.

I misfielded a couple of balls on the deep midwicket boundary. There's a bit of a ridge of turf just in front of the new stand, and it got into my head as I ran round to cut off a ball. So as I ran round I got my legs in a tangle, and the ball ricocheted off my foot for an extra run. I worried that my evening was going to consist of some poor fielding and a low score.

Rain reduced their innings to 34 overs and we were set a revised target of 152 in 25 overs, a target we were happy with. Sometimes the Duckworth-Lewis system can produce something unexpected, but I think the late wickets we got in their innings helped us.

Our opening effort was based around an excellent 43 from Will Jefferson. He seemed a lot more relaxed to me and played his power drives with aplomb. He strikes the ball as well as anyone, and it was a surprise when he mis-hit an attempted sweep off Gareth Breese to be caught on the long-on boundary. I had played very much a support role, but it was a pleasure to see Big Will playing so well.

Ashwell got out for one on debut, bringing Billy and me together. We both knew we needed a decent stand if we were to have any chance of scoring the eight and a bit runs per over to win.

We were doing really well, I'd hit Breese for a couple of sixes and Benkenstein for one as well. Then disaster. As I tried to swing a full toss to leg, my shoulder wrenched itself: it felt like it had popped out and then back in. Craig Smith, our physio, came out to check up on me. It's something I'd done a few times over the years, usually it just hurts for a while and then settles down. The slight problem is that the tendons and ligaments are stretched, making the shoulder feel lax and loose.

Fortunately it calmed down pretty quickly and I kept batting. It came down to 23 off 17 balls. Harmison came in to bowl at me, it was a low full toss which I tried to hit away to leg again but, as I was swinging through the shot, my shoulder went again. The ball ran away to fine leg, although I had no idea as all I could do is cradle my arm. This time I knew there was no chance of me carrying on. I just couldn't get my arm to move; it felt limp and unstable, as though it would pop again.

Craig came out again and asked me how it was. I told him what I thought, and he said I should come off. What greeted me in the changing room was genuinely unbelievable. Mick was stomping around, not looking at me in the eye, summoning Craig into his office. And, whilst this was going on, we proceeded to collapse. From needing 19 off 16 balls, with six wickets in hand, we managed to lose by six runs. It wasn't easy against Harmison, but we should still have won.

Beyond the result, Mick's behaviour was really concerning. He clearly thought I had come off not really injured, that I should have carried on. I was fuming. Craig had to calm me down in his office. He tried to explain that Mick was just caught up in the emotion of the game, that my departure had heralded the collapse and it was difficult for Mick to understand someone retiring hurt when he had never done so in his career.

But to me he was questioning my desire to win a game of cricket; he was questioning my commitment; and these accusations hurt. I even started to wonder whether I came off prematurely but, as soon as I tried to move my arm, I realised I would have had to have batted one-handed.

We lost the game, and the guys disbanded quickly. From being in a situation where we should have won and been in a great position in the table, we had lost and now everything was up for grabs again. The atmosphere was sour, with Mick storming around, not saying anything and the rest of the guys just quiet. Yet again I felt like the man everyone was blaming for the loss. I felt truly awful but immensely angry.

Mick came into the physio's room as I was getting some treatment. I said that I would never have left the field if I could have carried on – why on earth would I given up a chance to win the game for the team, the very best a single person can do? Mick explained his frustrations, and I could sympathise a bit. He said that all he could see was me coming off and us losing. If I had stayed on, then we would have won. I said that I would have had to have batted one-handed, I simply couldn't have moved my arm. I vented my anger to Rob when I got back home. It took me a while to calm down and get to sleep. What should have been a great night had turned into one to forget as soon as possible.

Wednesday 20 August

When I got to the ground Mick was waiting to have a chat. He was wearing his Mr Grumpy t-shirt, a present from some of the guys. Craig had told him that I wanted to meet up (I hadn't, but it was good of him to have arranged this). I explained how I felt, how the situation came across to me. Mick had calmed down, and we cleared the air. As ever I felt much better afterwards, but it is becoming something of a regular occurrence. I suppose it just takes some empathy: we are people of very different mentalities and at times find it hard to understand each others' responses to events. But ultimately I like Mick and I think, beneath the grumpy exterior, the feeling is reciprocated. I also think his regular bagging of me and my efforts is motivating, even if the emotional response is less beneficial. He is a good man who wears his heart on his sleeve.

This evening I spoke at the under-14 ESCA festival. Teams from the North, South, East and West regions all compete and an England team is picked at the end. I remember being very nervous and unsuccessful when I attended my festival. Philip Neville was playing, I seem to remember, and he had to decide between his football and cricket interests. I'm sure he regrets his decision everyday …

Hugh Cherry, a veteran organiser for whom I have a great deal of affection, said that I should offer some words of advice to the boys. I'm always reluctant to do so, given as I am to changes of belief and the fact that I'm hardly top of the tree. Nevertheless I actually enjoyed putting some thoughts together.

I had a great time, seated with David English, John Barclay and John Abrahams. The latter two had both coached me when I was younger. John B offered a very accurate assessment of me – it was easy to see why he was so highly regarded as a captain. We spoke about my plans post-cricket and what hopes I had for captaincy. He said that he thought it was something that I should seriously consider. He seemed to know exactly what would interest me. He was also the consummate MC, offering me an introduction of such quality and humour that my own efforts at oratory seemed pedestrian by comparison. Fortunately I think it went reasonably well.

I've always had latent ambitions of captaincy, ever since I enjoyed leading Oxford so much, but have put any hopes firmly on the back burner as circumstances have meant that it's never really been a feasible option. John also said that I shouldn't leave the move into the post-cricket career too late, that I should have energy and enthusiasm to throw into whatever it is I choose to do.

It was certainly stimulating stuff. Some people have the ability to enthuse and energise, and John and David are two of the best.

Thursday 21 August

Two treatment sessions today. The shoulder seems to be coming on well: the initial soreness has gone, and now it just feels a little loose in the joint. Gym involved some cycling and leg weights.

We have a few days before we go down to Hove on Tuesday. In fact, our fixtures are spread out quite nicely, with a few days between games.

Friday 22 August

More treatment, more gym and then time with the laptop. Disappointingly, I missed out on an hour's football at the ground today. I love playing our three-touch games, it's just a shame that football doesn't really love me. Ashwell is one of the best overseas players of football I've seen. Usually they have been brought up on rugby or Aussie rules and are therefore certainly inept with the spherical ball. Ash is skilled and is able to manufacture time on the ball. I shall have to ensure I'm always on his team as I think he could be the deciding factor in most of the games.

Chris and Matt Wood are also very good, although our captain has a slightly worrying predilection for trying to convince the referee that he has been fouled with outrageous displays of diving and wriggling around on the ground. Bringing up the rear is, well, me. Enthusiasm seems to have little impact on ball control, and will power evidently doesn't direct passes very well.

The season so far

County Championship – Division One

Canterbury	Kent	52		Won by 10 wickets
Headingley	Yorkshire	56		Drawn
Trent Bridge	Kent	42	21	Lost by 3 wickets
Trent Bridge	Lancashire	55	43*	Won by 7 wickets
Trent Bridge	Sussex	54	8	Lost by 73 runs
Old Trafford	Lancashire	94	0	Drawn
Southampton	Hampshire	66	67	Won by 6 wickets
Trent Bridge	Surrey	3	19	Drawn
Trent Bridge	Yorkshire	33	60	Won by 112 runs
Trent Bridge	Durham	2		Drawn
Taunton	Somerset	46	13	Drawn
Chester-le-Street	Durham	-		Abandoned, no play

M	Inn	NO	HS	Runs	Average	100s	50s
11	19	1	94	734	40.78	-	8

Table on 22 August

	P	W	L	D	Pts
Somerset	12	3	1	8	146
Nottinghamshire	12	4	2	6	137
Durham	11	5	2	4	136
Kent	12	4	4	4	133
Lancashire	12	3	2	7	126
Sussex	12	2	2	8	125
Hampshire	13	2	4	7	121
Yorkshire	12	2	5	5	116
Surrey	12	-	3	9	106

Friends Provident Trophy
Midland Group

Edgbaston	Warwickshire	-	Abandoned
Dublin	Ireland	0	Won by 56 runs
Trent Bridge	Northamptonshire	26	Won by 6 wickets
Trent Bridge	Leicestershire	37	Won by 2 wickets
Trent Bridge	Warwickshire	18	Lost by 52 runs
Northampton	Northamptonshire	-	Abandoned
Trent Bridge	Ireland	10	Won by 1 run
Oakham	Leicestershire	11	Lost by 13 runs

Quarter Final

Chester-le-Street	Durham	3	Lost by 1 wicket

M	Inn	NO	HS	Runs	Average	100s	50s
7	7	-	37	105	15.00	-	-

Pro-40 League – Division One

Worcester	Worcestershire	7	Won by 6 wickets
Trent Bridge	Hampshire	2	Won by 31 runs
Cheltenham	Gloucestershire	28	Won by 9 runs
Taunton	Somerset	34	Lost by 3 wickets
Trent Bridge	Durham	50*	Lost by 6 runs

M	Inn	NO	HS	Runs	Average	100s	50s
5	5	1	50*	121	30.25	-	1

Table on 22 August

	P	W	L	NR	Pts
Nottinghamshire	5	3	2	-	6
Gloucestershire	5	2	1	2	6
Sussex	5	2	1	2	6
Hampshire	5	2	2	1	5
Durham	4	2	2	-	4
Somerset	6	2	4	-	4
Worcestershire	3	1	1	1	3
Middlesex	3	1	1	1	3
Lancashire	4	-	1	3	3

Chapter Eleven

The excitement is mounting

This is building into one of the most exciting seasons of recent memory. There is a real belief that anything is possible. I seem to have settled into some decent form, and I'm delighted that I have reacted positively to the Twenty20 situation. I've talked about the idea of discovering aspects of myself and my game, seeing what I do in various circumstances. Talk is so often cheap, and it's actions that count. Hence my pleasure with my form in the last few weeks.

As a team we have a real belief in our method: our ability to score enough runs and the firepower of our attack to take wickets. Looking ahead towards the last month of the season, every deed will matter. The eventual winners, in addition to excellent performances, will have been blessed with good luck with respect to injuries and weather.

When I look round our team I have a lot of faith in our abilities. That doesn't mean that I think we'll win every session, but it means that we are more than capable of doing well in a lot of situations.

It's becoming more normal now to refer to tables, and the closeness of combatants just motivates. We are second in the Championship behind Somerset and just ahead of Durham. They have both been playing good cricket and have some very good performers. We will need to be excellent for much of this coming month.

The Pro40, of which we are top, is open to anyone. At least we are in pole position. I feel a little less confident of our prospects in this competition as I think we have displayed a brittleness at times. We have also been very powerful, but it's that weakness which worries me. And, of course, in this shortened format one poor session can cost you the game and with it the league.

Chapter Twelve

The closing weeks

Tuesday 26 August

It's a noticeable feature that the boys have been looking at tables a lot more in the last few days. I think I've looked at the Pro40 every day and thought about what would be the situation if we had won last week. I drove Ashwell Prince down here to Brighton. In the car he was checking out the leagues.

Four hours in a car is usually a long time. However, I really enjoyed the trip down and the time passed quickly. The one thing that struck me about Ashwell is that he is a fiercely determined guy, and I can see why he is vice-captain of the South Africans. I think he'll bring some backbone to our batting in the last month of the season.

We are playing five bowlers this week, with Andre missing out and Paul Franks playing to bolster the batting as well as take wickets. It must have been a difficult decision to leave Andre out as he has been excellent with the ball this year. Paul, though, has offered with the bat virtually every time he has played, and his lower-order runs may be crucial. He also has the ability to get a wicket from nowhere, which may be a vital asset on what are generally slow low wickets here at Hove. Mick, Chris and Mark were in deep discussion for a while, pacing up and down the wicket, reading the runes. These decisions can make or break a season, and they were clearly intent on making a well thought out decision.

I'm also pleased to say that Rob Ferley is getting a game. The net wickets spun square so he should get at least some assistance from the pitch. It certainly looks as though it will deteriorate, with the surface already consisting of a series of 'plates' moving slightly to the touch.

Ash spoke at the team meeting about scoring 500 or 600 and putting them under pressure. The rest of us looked around and tried to suppress a cheeky smile: we haven't exactly been knocking on the door of 300s, let alone anything bigger. Positivity, though, and the power of thinking big and all that ...

On the international stage, it was slightly heartening to see the South African batters struggling at TB in the one-day international – at least it's not just us. To be fair, the wicket looked pretty good, it seemed to be bounce and good bowling that undid the Springboks. Samit played ahead of Graeme again. I bumped into Swanny on Saturday, and he was understandably despondent. It's an astonishing rise for Samit, and he deserves a great deal of credit and respect. I've remarked in this diary how he is a very confident young man, and his self-belief has paid off.

Wednesday 27 August
Hove, County Championship – Day One
Sussex 292 for five

We lost the toss. I hope that this won't be crucial, but the wicket is already taking spin and it looks like it is only going to get worse. The ball didn't do a great deal, a little when it was new was the best it offered. It was attritional cricket for much of the day, each side trying to grind to an advantage.

Every session is important and tomorrow morning's will be no exception. We need a couple of early wickets whilst they will be looking to move towards 400 to 450. A point Mick made yesterday I think is particularly apt. He said that winning the championship would involve playing and succeeding in conditions that were a little foreign. This slow, spinning wicket is a long way from the TB surface, and it will require imagination for us to find ways to get wickets and patience and perseverance when we come to bat.

I spent most of the day patrolling the boundaries. I felt a bit handicapped with my shoulder, not being able to move it freely with confidence. I misfielded one horribly when backing up a slightly errant throw when I couldn't get my left arm down in time. Fielding is hard enough at the best of times, but being reduced effectively to one arm was pretty difficult to say the least!

Mark Ealham picked up three wickets on his 39th birthday. He arrived at the ground slightly deflated this morning. He was hoping for a laptop for his present but instead received a chopping board and vegetable cutter. It was the identical shape as well, apparently, but when he picked it up and felt the weight he was a little suspicious. I would have loved to see his face when he took the wrapping paper off; I bet it was priceless!

Thursday 28 August
Hove, County Championship – Day Two
Sussex 339 all out (Shreck 4-82)
Nottinghamshire 259 for two (Shafayat 118, Jefferson 80, Wagh 31)*

Today couldn't have gone much better. We ran through the last five wickets with relative ease, and then Will and Billy played wonderfully well to leave us in a very good position.

It started with Charlie bowling with real potency on a very flat wicket. He has taken 50 wickets now this season, which underlines his talent and consistency. Then Billy and Will not only played with solidity but also with aggression, popping sixes and fours against their spinners, which has given us an excellent edge in this contest.

At tea time there was a presentation to Mushtaq Ahmed. It involved a trumpet fanfare, a tearful valediction from Chris Adams and words from the man himself. The Sussex faithful clearly hold Mushy close to their hearts. What Mushy has shown more than anything else is that successful teams need a touch of magic. On these turning pitches at Hove, he was the King, taking wickets with ease. On the back of his sterling efforts, reputations and careers have been enhanced and furthered. The genius lay in the initial signing. To take a former international, with a questionable fitness record, who was playing club cricket, and see the potential was brilliant.

Whilst we were watching the pageantry, I mentioned, tongue firmly in cheek, to Mark that this would be for him next year. Paul Franks was nominated as the deliverer of the tearful farewell. Something on this scale, however, would be laughably incongruous to Ealy as a man. He is self-deprecating, understated and is a reluctant inhabiter of the limelight.

This evening newcomer Alex Hales organised the team meal. He was a tad nervous, to say the least. It's an unforgiving audience when it comes to food: Ealham in particular very picky when it comes to affairs of gustation. Alex did well, though, and made a very acceptable post-meal speech. We are trying to break the £1,000 mark for the bill on these occasions, with our next effort in London being our best hope for the season. I'm not the most enthusiastic attendee of these meals usually, but this was a good one and very enjoyable.

Friday 29 August
Hove, County Championship – Day Three
Sussex 339 & 7 for no wicket
Nottinghamshire 558 for seven, dec (Wagh 128, Shafayat 118, Wood 98, Jefferson 80)

A run-fest at Hove. It was pleasing to get my first century of the year, even if it's taken me this long to get there. It was a piece of brain-dead thinking that got me out – trying to slog one when all I needed to do was knock it around. I'm focussed on chasing down the runs I need to get to 1,000 for the year. Given the wickets we've had at TB, I'll be happy to get past that milestone. I think I now need another 150 or so.

Usually scoring a hundred gives an amazing sense of satisfaction. However, in these circumstances, with virtually everyone getting some runs, I'm just happy that I haven't missed out and have contributed to the team effort. I'm left feeling pleased with my innings but no more.

Matt played a very aesthetically pleasing knock. It's a strange sensation to get out just short of a century. Initially it's abject disappointment, falling so close to such an important land mark. But that subsides and a warm sense of achievement takes over.

It's going be hard work for us tomorrow but it's funny how sometimes a team can subside under a bit of pressure. We were given a little fillip when we heard that Hampshire had beaten Durham. Sean Ervine played well to see his team home. Durham and Somerset are still the teams most likely to win, having a game in hand over us, but we are very close behind.

Saturday 30 August
Hove, County Championship – Day Four
Sussex 339 & 243 for three
Nottinghamshire 558 for seven, declared
Match drawn

I have a feeling I've said this before, but today was a terribly dull day. The car park attendant said it would be, and he was spot on. We never looked like taking ten wickets, faced as we were with steadfast batting and a pitch which gave our seamers nothing. We tried but in vain. These games should be called off at tea as the post-tea hour is a sight that does no favours to the game, with non-bowlers wheeling away and no one particularly interested.

Charlie had a real go early on, getting the first wicket, but he couldn't shift Yardy which would have opened it up a little. On such an unresponsive surface it was a fine spell of bowling.

Even I got a bowl, although my body is not thanking me for it. I haven't bowled for twelve months, and nine overs have ensured that it will be at least another year before I have another spell. When I bowl I hyperextend my elbow; it bends backwards. For most of my life, everyone has thought I throw the ball when I bowl. This came to a head a few years ago when, during a live televised game, Ronnie Irani, the Essex captain, made a hoohah during an over. The umpires got together and, rather than calling me for throwing, asked the captain to take me off. It's always bemused me as to why Ronnie did that, given that I was no threat to his wicket and he was happily taking me for four an over.

Nevertheless, a couple of weeks later, the ECB sent up Bob Carter to video my action and they decided that I needed to correct it in order to bowl again. I discovered at the subsequent hearing that this video had me in silhouette so it was completely impossible to see what my body parts were doing. And in the Sky footage I was in a long-sleeve shirt. It was shabby administration in my opinion but, as it turned out, it provided me with a valuable opportunity to get to the bottom of my action.

I spent the next couple of months trying to work out what was going on. Looking at it at normal speed, I could only think that I bent my

Chris Read, one of the most effective death batsmen, hits another six.

Mister Grumpy, Charlie Shreck, doing what he loves most.

Strong as an ox, Andre Adams is a key figure.

Matt Wood accepts the congratulations for a fine running catch.

No, don't touch! The shoulder's gone.

A good day at The Oval. Samit and I put on 242.

At The Oval. On the way to scoring my 1,000th run.

It was supposed to be a photo of the crowd celebrating.
The last ball of the Pro40 match against Sussex.

A long day in the field against Hampshire.
The championship title is starting to seem a long way away.

Back in the changing room. Writing this diary.

elbow. I videoed from all angles, tried different actions, but each time it just looked like I threw it. I was losing hope, but then I had the 'Eureka' moment. I decided that I would try a real close-up of the elbow at super-slow motion. When I reviewed the footage, I realised why it looked like the elbow was bent – because it was. But rather than being bent like a throw, it bent backwards. This, coupled with a very flexible shoulder joint, meant that I was leading with my hyper-extended elbow joint, which makes it look like I'm throwing the ball.

I had to go down to Lord's to a 20-man throwing committee. They looked at the previous footage, then they listened to what I had to say and viewed the footage I had taken, backed up with medical testimony regarding the hyper-flexibility in my joints. Then I was excused, and they discussed the evidence. I was staying in a local hotel, and I remember the intervening hours as being very tense. Eventually I received a call clearing my action and allowing me to bowl. It was an enormous relief. And a real sense of achievement.

The process had given me a far greater understanding of my action than I would otherwise have had and gave me the opportunity to experience a throwing committee hearing.

Sunday 31 August

Recovery and then a benefit match in Tintwistle for AJ Harris. The three-hour return journey was a fitting end to a fairly ordinary day. It had rained continuously during the game, and the guys were grumpy and tired. The locals fortunately offered excellent hospitality.

It looks like the Universities are going to lose their first-class status. I can't say I'm that surprised as, ever since they expanded the system in the light of political correctness, this was a likely outcome. The old Oxbridge situation was a typically English anachronism, quirky yet it worked in a fashion. Of course a group of students are never going to be on the same level as a professional team, and conferring the same status to them is ridiculous. It was possible to accept when there were only two teams, but expanded to four the illogicality was highlighted.

I was sad when the first-class badge was offered to more universities but now, distanced by years, this final culling elicits little emotion from me. Nevertheless, it will be sad to see the Parks and Fenner's effectively rot. But even they aren't the same places I remember, full as they are of non-University players. This might all sound elitist, and indeed it is. But not all such things are bad; equality can sometimes mean making it worse for everyone.

Tuesday 2 September

The speedy passage of the season is something that always amazes me. I can't believe we're into early starts and the nights are closing in. Usually the cooler weather and autumnal feel don't inspire but this year, with the run-in keeping everyone interested, I'm pretty excited.

There's no need for me to go on about the importance of this game against Somerset. I'll just reproduce the table:

	P	W	L	D	Pts
Nottinghamshire	13	4	2	7	149
Somerset	12	3	1	8	146
Kent	13	4	4	5	140
Durham	12	5	3	4	139
Hampshire	14	3	4	7	138
Sussex	13	2	2	9	133
Lancashire	13	3	2	8	130
Yorkshire	13	2	5	6	128
Surrey	13	-	3	10	110

We are hopeful that Graeme will come back and join us from Thursday onwards. Of course it's been a terribly disappointing one-day series for him, and it will be a test to see how he responds to this return to the ranks. The knock-on effect has meant that Rob has been dropped. He is very despondent and needs some time to think through his position. His one-day performances for us have been excellent, but in the limited four-day opportunities he's had he hasn't quite hit his straps. It's a bit of a Catch 22 situation: he can't get better at four-day cricket without playing, but he won't play unless he gets better.

I visited a surgeon this evening, to be told that I need an operation to repair my shoulder. Apparently, it is beyond loose and is now unstable. And I've got four months of rehab to look forward to. It's a bit out of the blue, and I'm going to get a second opinion. I suspect there will be no alternative, but it makes sense at least to get confirmation. It feels as though my shoulder could pop out at any stage, and it's been a couple of weeks since the Durham game so it looks like something needs to be done. Surgery is always a last resort, with its associated risks, but I'm not sure I have any other option.

Wednesday 3 September

Trent Bridge, County Championship – Day One
Somerset 143 for seven

Justin Langer is a superb player, but today won't make it into his top ten cricket days. First, he won the toss and decided to bat, a choice that raised a few eyebrows. Then he strode out to face the first ball of the innings but was forced to stride straight back, having kicked a straight one from Charlie. Everyone knows the exceptional quality Somerset have at the top of the order so early wickets are like gold. On the hour, Andre removed Trescothick's off stump, having watched him middle every ball he had faced to that point. There followed a middle-order crumble and, despite some later resistance, it left us in a strong position.

Rain has frustrated our efforts today, with no play after 3 p.m. The ground is really wet, and I'm not sure if we will start on time tomorrow. The club are intending to dig up the outfield over the winter and install a sand-based one which should allow any rain to drain away. It will mean that, as soon as it stops raining, we should be able to get back on the park comparatively quickly. It could be a crucial ingredient if the weather is as inclement next year.

As for other news: Mark Ealham has just got a new laptop. It's a very shiny affair, but he seems very pleased with it; I'm seeing another consultant next week to get a second opinion, he has the brilliant name of Dr Funk. Paul Franks has been laid low with a virus.

Thursday 4 September

Trent Bridge, County Championship – Day Two
Somerset 252 all out
Nottinghamshire 46 for two (Wagh 1*)

Late-wicket partnerships are amongst the most frustrating experiences for the fielding team. After taking the eighth wicket in the third over of the day, we were hopeful of a straightforward wrap-up. Peter Trego and Andy Caddick had other ideas and, with Trego swashbuckling at one end and Caddick stonewalling at the other, we just couldn't get a wicket and they were scoring at will. Thankfully Graeme came on and beat Trego in the air, causing him to spoon it to me at deep midwicket. My heart was in my mouth as the ball came down towards me, but it hit my hands and stuck. Relief!

The afternoon was spoiled by rain. We played a little and lost Will and Andre, who batted as night-watchman. I can't believe how much rain we are having this summer.

Friday 5 September

Trent Bridge, County Championship – Day Three
No play

Guess what? It rained all day. It seems that there is no end to this year's rainfall. I had a massage at lunch time and the ground was almost one big puddle (I suppose that makes it a lake), so with all the rain this afternoon and that scheduled overnight, it must make tomorrow's prospects grim. This Championship could come down to who avoids the rain the best.

Mick sent a text round, telling us not to come to the ground. So it was gym, lunch and cinema today. I went with Chris and Mark to watch the latest Guy Ritchie film, *Rockanrolla*. Ealy was keen to see the third Mummy film ("It'll be rubbish," came the cries), Chris was all for a bit of Step Brothers ("It'll be rubbish," said Ealy) but consensus was reached eventually.

Saturday 6 September

Trent Bridge, County Championship – Day Four
No play, match drawn

No surprises this morning. We arrived at the ground just to shake hands with the Somerset boys and wish them all the best for the rest of season (nothing could be further from our true hopes, of course). The management decided a gym session was called for, which went down as well as you would expect with the bowlers. Then on the road down south through heavy, ponderous showers.

This coming week is crucial for our season. We are playing our final three Pro40 games which, if we win them, will mean we will be champions. And Somerset play Durham over four days. The best result is for rain and points shared. Probably the worst result is for Somerset to win with bonus points. The game is being played in Chester-le-Street which means a result would be likely if the weather were to hold, but it is also very likely that rain could have a major input. There will be some anxious scanning of forecasts this week.

Tomorrow's game against Middlesex sees the return of Graeme and Samit, the latter clearly buoyed by his performances in the last few weeks. We are as strong as we can realistically be and will be a formidable challenge for Middlesex. But they are Twenty20 champions, of course, so it should be an excellent game. It would appear that they have a few issues regarding the captaincy to sort out. I've remarked a number of times how sport is cyclical, with its phases of success, stagnation and rejuvenation. The rebuilding phase can be traumatic, but is an inevitable part of the process.

I think it is possible to catalyse it by buying in players who are in the appropriate stage of their development. It still takes skill to marry together the right set of players and to foresee what the club will need in a year or two's time. Of course this is more prevalent in football whilst, in cricket, squads tend to morph less so greater foresight is required.

I was involved in the stagnation and rebuilding phases at Warwickshire when I started playing in 1998. The wonder team of '94 were coming to the end but were understandably keen to keep playing as long as possible. The rejuvenation was a long, drawn-out affair and it is only this season that it looks like they are coming through the dark tunnel. They have a good man in charge in Ashley Giles, and he is leading them well.

Monday 8 September

Lord's, Pro40 League
Nottinghamshire 180 all out (Wagh 1)
Middlesex 161 all out
Nottinghamshire won by 19 runs

There was a real buzz around the changing room after the game. We had won, despite scoring 180 at Lord's, with a sparkling bowling performance and not inconsiderable help from the Middlesex batsmen.

It was a wintry day: cold, blustery with heavy, threatening cloud cover. I doubt we would have played much if it had been a championship game, given that the light was appalling for most of proceedings. I was grateful that this game was important to us because in these conditions the best use for a bit of willow is a roaring fire accompanied by a hot drink.

We started well with Will and Graeme adding 57 for the first wicket. But, as the first batch of rain came through, we bizarrely stayed on despite its becoming heavy for a while. The wicket spiced up, started to nip around off the seam, and we struggled to get to 180. Their spinners, Udal and Kartik, got some purchase, which is something you don't often see here.

It was a 'working total': not great but enough to give us a chance. Charlie Shreck started off and bowled excellently. With Andre at the other end getting the key wicket of Andy Strauss, we were in the hunt. These first few overs of each innings turned out to be crucial: we scored 50-odd, whilst they lost three wickets.

Owais Shah is a brilliant player and pivotal for Middlesex. So, when Mark Ealham trapped him lbw, we were ecstatic. What followed was a succession of batters getting in and then out. They played as if they were chasing eight an over rather than the four or five which it was for most of their innings.

This shouldn't diminish the efforts of Graeme. His analysis of 7-0-27-3 was a true reflection of the skill and guile with which he bowled. I've said it before, but he is a class act.

We are now in a great position in this Pro40. Of course I can't help thinking about that Durham game again …

Tuesday 9 September

We could have a very wealthy dressing room next year. Graeme, Samit, Stuart and Ryan are all in the squad to play in the Stanford game in November. I think there is an air of the unreal about it at the moment – show-me-the-money-and-I'll-believe-it. The idea of having $1,000,000 deposited in your account is extraordinary for most people. They all seem fairly philosophical about the venture, shrugging shoulders at the idea, seeing the money as an unexpected bonus: desperately trying, I imagine, not to give in to the wonderful possibilities of winning so much money and then losing the game.

Tomorrow's Pro40 game against Lancashire is next on the list. If we win and Sussex lose to Middlesex on Thursday, we will be crowned champions. The ground is soaking wet, but we will be doing everything possible to play. With a decent forecast I think we will be OK.

Lancashire are an interesting team. They have consistently over the last few years been the bridesmaid, never quite making it up the aisle themselves. And it's not for lack of talent or application. At the moment they seem to have some issues with the release of Dominic Cork, a move opposed by the captain and their superstar Andy Flintoff. It's difficult to say how off-field events can impact on performance on it, but it does seem to have some kind of malign influence.

Somerset are playing Durham in Taunton this week. Today's play was washed out which is obviously great for us. A low-scoring draw with few wickets please…

Wednesday 10 September

Lord's, Pro40 League
Lancashire 202 for eight (Patel 3-34)
Nottinghamshire 201 all out (Swann 61, Wagh 9)
Lancashire won by 1 run

Another truly awful day. There was anger from Mick after the game about the efforts of us batters. Needing less than five an over with nine wickets in hand should have been a breeze. Instead, we managed to lose this crucial fixture.

The wicket spun as much as any wicket I've seen at TB. But it wasn't their spinner who caused us the problems; it was the medium-pace bowling of Croft and Smith.

Criticism of the bowlers has been a rare occurrence in this diary; they have performed time and again this season. But I don't think we did as well as we could. We bowled a fair few deliveries that were easily put away. Nevertheless, our reply started brilliantly; the in-form Graeme Swann smashed 61 off 42 balls, obliterating any run rate concerns and putting the Lancastrians firmly on the back foot. When he got out, we needed less than 120 runs to win. Then …

I got a thin edge to an innocuous delivery, Ashwell was unlucky to be given lbw, and Samit nicked one behind. And that was our middle order. 19 runs, 44 balls. You can see where Mick's venomous blast was coming from. Of course, whether that actually helped us is another matter.

A heartfelt dressing down, the old-fashioned kick up the backside, definitely has a role to play in man management – although the frequency and timing are crucial. If as a player you're trying your best, then it can simply antagonise after a while. Will power alone doesn't produce results, and a lack of results doesn't mean a lack of desire or commitment. As a bowler, if things aren't going for you, there is always the physical exertion to show that you care, that you are doing everything you can. Batsmen don't have that opportunity. If you make a mistake, you walk off and sit in the pavilion. There's no sweat, no pain, nothing: it looks like you've just not tried.

And here's the Catch 22: the harder you try, the more you want to show how much you care, the less chance there is that you will bat well. That relaxed state of mind where instincts take over and the body does what it does best, is most hindered when tense, desperate, effortful.

Unsurprisingly, it was a morose dressing room after play. I retreated to the pub and a couple of pints. It's not a normal recourse for me, but I needed to dull the sting from the performance and Mick's words.

Thursday 11 September

I felt a little uneasy at recovery this morning. I don't know if I was just projecting what I felt onto other people, but it seemed there were a few accusatory looks; there certainly wasn't much bonhomie.

I had a bowling machine session with Mick. Not much bonhomie there, either. I certainly didn't want to mention last night or anything to do with it. And I was reluctant to ask what the plans were for tomorrow and Saturday as he had jumped down my throat when I asked yesterday between innings.

Saturday 13 September

We are poised on the cusp over which our season will be decided. Let's deal with the Championship first.

	P	W	L	D	Pts
Hampshire	15	4	4	7	160
Somerset	14	3	1	10	159
Durham	14	5	3	6	157
Nottinghamshire	14	4	2	8	156
Kent	14	4	4	6	147
Sussex	14	2	2	10	141
Lancashire	14	3	2	9	135
Yorkshire	14	2	5	7	135
Surrey	15	-	4	11	119

I think it shows how close this year's competition has been when a team who were close to bottom just a few weeks ago are now top. Hampshire are showing a late resurgence, a sharp reversal in fortune that seems to coincide with the appointment of Giles White as coach. Impossible to say, of course, how directly correlated the two things are, but it would support one of the themes of this diary that a settled environment off the pitch aids performance on it.

Then come the three teams that have consistently been in the running: Somerset, Durham and us. Thanks to a draw this week in Taunton, we are all neck and neck. And Kent can't be discounted, either. It's a shame that much of the media's sporting coverage will be dominated as ever by football.

But today most of my thoughts are on tomorrow's game against Sussex in the Pro40. The winner takes it all. It turns out our loss on Wednesday was irrelevant since Sussex beat Middlesex the following day. So it comes down to a shoot-out at our place. Sussex are a very good side: Prior and Goodwin the principal batsmen, Luke Wright offering fireworks with both bat and ball, and a well-disciplined bowling attack led by Mohammed Sami and James Kirtley.

Practice yesterday concluded with a constructive chat amongst the middle order about our roles and strengths in one-day cricket. Mick wanted us to say what we brought to the team so that everyone understood what we were trying to do when we were out there in the middle. It also looks like we are changing the order a bit: Samit will come in at three if we are going well at the start to take advantage of the restrictions; otherwise he will bat four, allowing Ashwell to run the ball around in the middle period.

Sunday 14 September

Trent Bridge, Pro40 League
Nottinghamshire 226 for seven (Patel 78, Wagh 8)
Sussex 229 for eight (Goodwin 87*, Swann 3-33, Patel 3-36)
Sussex won by two wickets

There was an eerie silence just after Murray Goodwin struck the final ball of the innings. It was pure disbelief. But, as it sailed ever higher, the first wave of realisation came from the Sussex balcony, lone jubilant voices cheering the ball on its winning parabola. Then the crowd: hysteria from the Sussex supporters, raucously hailing their hero. I'm not sure what my first reaction was. I had been concentrating on what my role would be if the ball (gulp!) came to me. "Just watch the ball into your hands, take your time and get it in." It took me a moment to realise that it wasn't coming to me, then that it was going for six, and then slowly, as the Sussex voices carried across the ground, it dawned on me that we had lost the unlosable.

For the vast majority of the game we were winning. I'm not sure if Mick and Chris knew quite how much the wicket was going to spin later in the day but, if it was a plan, it worked a treat. We won the toss, batted and posted an above-average score that we would have taken before the game.

The batting hero was Samit who struck a wristy, belligerent 78. It could have been very different if Mohammed Sami had caught a relatively straightforward chance at fine leg. Instead, the ball came out of the sun and hit him on his flank. In these games it is such chances that give the lucky recipients the belief that today is their day and Samit went on to play some lovely shots. He had the Sussex attack at his feet when he drilled one to long off.

I was disappointing again. Against some tight bowling I didn't want just to sit there and let them bowl at me. So I wandered down the wicket and played a straight-legged push at a James Kirtley delivery that I sliced to backward point. I was trying to hit it through mid-on. If only I had hit it straight. All the frustrations and pain hit me as I walked off. I felt like hurling the bat through the changing room. My one-day season has been atrocious, and I need some time to sit down and work out where I'm going from here. No doubt my appraisal with Mick will hammer home this point.

Defending 226 (average score in the Pro40 at TB: 195), we got a couple of crucial early wickets in Prior and Luke Wright. But then Yardy and Adams played well, and we were reduced to damage limitation with the white ball doing little off the surface. We needed to get the spinners involved as soon as we could. And true to form, it all changed when

Graeme and Samit started bowling. With prodigious spin, especially from Graeme, and excellent control from them both, we reduced Sussex to 130 for eight.

From that point of apparent domination, it was all Murray Goodwin. 87 from 64 balls, 6 fours and 3 sixes. But it was the manner in which he seemed completely in control of the situation that most impressed me. He received vital support from Sami (32 off 25 balls) without whom Murray's efforts would have been in vain. It's funny how TB can seem such a small ground when someone has his eye in, today being the perfect example.

Usually a chase of ten an over generates some chances, a spooned catch, a wild swipe. But not this time. It was as clinical as you can get. Murray and Chris Adams were exceedingly gracious in their post-match interviews. Murray in particular took the plaudits with humour and a laudable helping of self-deprecation.

Chris announced his resignation from the Sussex captaincy after eleven years in charge. Just to stay at the helm for as long as he has is a superb achievement, but to win five trophies is a really tremendous feat. A county dressing room can be a cruel place; reputations ebb and flow with the seasons. To retain the respect of his fellow players for such a long period is exceptional.

I felt a bit numb after the game and very, very tired. Total disappointment at the result, my (lack of) contribution, all that effort for nothing. Swanny, somehow, played a gig with his group. I was just exhausted, absolutely spent. I aimlessly surfed the net and then wrote this.

Tuesday 16 September

Two games to go, championship up for grabs.

Back on the road. This time down to the Oval, Matt Wood in the driver's seat. There are two issues this week: Ramprakash and us. The first is self-evident: we need to get this master out twice. Enough said. The second issue is more interesting. We need to be a team looking forwards, supporting each other's efforts, determined to win. I think there is a tension in the changing room at the moment. I feel it will be interesting to see how we react if events start going against us over these two weeks. We will need to support each other, not descend into recrimination and finger pointing.

Losing has this habit of exposing cracks. We lost four of our last five Pro40 games and our last Championship win was Yorkshire: our momentum is poor. Mick's chastisement of the batters the other day has left me feeling as though I'm battling not only the opposition but trying to avoid the finger of blame on return to the dressing room. Part of me just wants the season to end. I hope that this afternoon's training session dispels this rather morose gloom. All it will take is a comment, a lightness of spirit to lift things and put me back on track.

Perhaps I'm just being unrealistic. We are cricketers, paid to perform. Don't perform and expect to be criticised. Stop being such a sissy! All true, and I completely agree. How can I expect people to say 'well played' if I'm not prepared for them to have their say if I play poorly?

I also feel like I've let Mick and Chris down. Their consistent selection has been excellent and, when I fail to deliver, I'm putting them in a difficult position when those out of the team come knocking, wondering why they are not playing.

Wednesday 17 September
The Oval, County Championship – Day One
Surrey 253 for eight

The Oval is a superb stadium. The imposing OCS stand, with its sweeping arch, and the beautiful brick pavilion at the opposite end offer opposing examples of architectural design. Sitting high up in the new changing rooms, looking down on the play, there's an amphitheatre feel to the ground, and I can only imagine what it must be like to play to a full house. The Millennium Wheel turns in the background, and the Houses of Parliament can just be seen through the arch. It's a big club in a big city.

We lost the toss and bowled; everyone wanted to bat. Autumn seems to have thudded into the year, with chilly, dewy mornings and thin, watery sunshine. The first hour was like a limited-overs game with Scott Newman playing some crisp drives, bringing up his 50 and looking threatening. The rest of the day couldn't have provided a much greater contrast, with a tedious run rate and a slow but vital trickle of wickets. Charlie Shreck got the most precious wicket of Ramprakash with a beauty that just feathered the outside edge. I felt like throwing a party; he's scored so many big hundreds that he can sentence you to what feels like days in the field.

Darren Pattinson came through a fitness test this morning on a troublesome groin injury. We have been remarkably fortunate in keeping our bowlers on the park this summer, in comparison to last year when even the bowlers we signed on loan got injured.

We are in an excellent position on this easy-paced batting friendly wicket. Plan A will be to get them out first thing tomorrow, put a big total on the board and apply as much pressure second innings as possible.

Today's play also confirmed that Surrey would be relegated to the second division. I read in the papers over the weekend that they are looking for a complete rejuvenation package with the Stephens, Fleming and Waugh, mentioned as the dream ticket. They certainly have the budget to attract most of the game's luminaries. I think it will be a long-term project as a club's fortunes rarely turn on a sixpence. But, given the resources available to whoever takes over, the potential is obvious.

Thursday 18 September

The Oval, County Championship – Day Two
Surrey 267 all out (Adams 4-40)
Nottinghamshire 420 for five (Wagh 141, Patel 135)

It's rare for a day to go quite so according to plan. We polished off the final couple of wickets, then Samit and I put on almost 250, leaving us in a perfect position.

Samit was magnificent, dispatching the bowlers as though they weren't even on the same plane as him. I haven't seen a batsman score so freely for a long time. He only faced 121 deliveries, and it was a pleasure to watch from the other end. It was so evident that the confidence that he has gleaned from playing international cricket is catapulting his county form into a different class. He is in with a great chance of picking up the PCA's Most Valuable Player award which would be a fitting end to a fine season.

On a personal note I passed 1,000 runs during this innings. I've mentioned how that milestone this year would have special significance for me, given the difficulty of scoring runs at TB. At least I can look back at this season with some sense of achievement and, if we do go on to win the Championship, I can say that I contributed.

I also faced Shoaib Akhtar. Often the first question I get from cricket fans goes along the lines of "Have you faced Shane Warne/ Brett Lee/ Shaoib Akhtar?" and I have had to answer negatively to the last two. Unfortunately I don't think I can claim to have faced the Rawalpindi Express at his fiercest, but I got a taste of the theatre and drama of what it must be like. He sprints in from what seems an inordinate distance huffing, puffing, sometimes saying something to you on the way, there's a whirlwind of arms and from the chaos comes a rocket accompanied by a grunt, scream or yelp. It's magnificent to watch and great to be involved in.

I watched Mark Ramprakash during warm-ups. He showed no signs of fatigue or despondency. During the day he was vocal, involved and committed. I wonder what motivates him on a day like today. I can easily understand the practically innate desire to score runs. But the fervour with which he threw himself around in the field, on a sunk ship, in front of a handful of spectators, points to an exceptionally high degree of motivation. Just what it is (personal pride? not wanting to let the team down? wanting to set the example?) is anyone's guess.

Friday 19 September

The Oval, County Championship – Day Three
Surrey 267 & 122 all out
Nottinghamshire 532 all out
Nottinghamshire won by an innings and 143 runs

I was both delighted to win this game and then almost instantly a bit nervous about what it means. With both Durham and Somerset looking as if they are going to draw their games, we will be about eight points clear at the top of the table going into the final game. We are so close ....

But back to today. With the team that Surrey put out for this game, they needed their best players to fire to allow the younger guys to play supporting roles. When their senior players didn't do that, there was every chance that we could run through them. And that is exactly what happened. It looked likely at one stage that we would bowl them out in a session, a pretty damning indication of the level of application on this belting wicket.

I can't blame them, though. Relegated and no doubt wanting to forget this season as quickly as possible, a battling rearguard action was unlikely.

All the action this week has been against the backdrop of the drama in the financial markets. Being in London, a lot of the guys are catching up with friends who are directly affected by the bankruptcies, mergers and subsequent job losses. We are getting an idea of the sheer uncertainty running through the London community at the moment. There's something quintessentially English sitting high up in the changing rooms watching a group of men in white chase a leather ball around a field, gently applauded by a smattering of ageing citizens, whilst just over the back of the stand the modern world is being brought to its knees because of complex financial products.

Monday 22 September

Here's the table:

	P	W	L	D	Pts
Nottinghamshire	15	5	2	8	178
Somerset	15	3	1	11	170
Durham	15	5	3	7	168
Hampshire	15	4	4	7	160
Lancashire	15	4	2	9	152
Kent	15	4	5	6	151
Sussex	15	2	2	11	151
Yorkshire	15	2	5	8	147
Surrey	16	-	5	11	124

One more game, one solid performance and the Championship is ours. I'm not sure exactly how many weeks we have topped the table, but it feels as if we have been there or thereabouts for the majority of this season. I can't pretend that I'm not worried that we are going to fall at the final hurdle – the requirement of only needing a good draw might make us timid, fretful. I'm sure, if events do take a turn for the worse, there will be some understandable nervousness. But my gut feel (hostage to fortune here) is that we will be OK. In my mind's eye, I can see Charlie and Darren steaming in taking wickets, leading the charge. We are at home, difficult though it has been at times, so we are on familiar territory.

Hampshire, we think, will have their star spinner, Imran Tahir, so there is a very good chance that every blade of grass will be left on the wicket. They had claimed that he has left to return to South Africa, but Mick thinks he is around and will play. A little gamesmanship just adds to the week ….

Hampshire have a mathematical chance to win, but I wonder how they will play if that chance disappears. Durham and Somerset are playing Kent and Lancashire respectively, teams desperately fighting to retain Division One status. These speculative ramblings are indicative of my trying to think through every angle rather than just concentrating on the one thing that matters: playing well. No doubt that message will be central to the team talk tomorrow at practice.

I'm on the way to Manchester to get a second opinion on my shoulder. The scan I had last week has highlighted a torn cartilage, and Craig is fairly sure I will need to get it repaired to ensure it doesn't happen again. The four months of rehab, and the subsequent effort to recover aerobic and muscular fitness, is not exactly an appealing thought. Usually I see the winter as a chance to take my game forward, but it would seem my efforts this time will be directed to ensuring that I start next season in no worse condition than I started this one.

Tuesday 23 September
Low key practice, the wind and drizzle combined with a chill, give the morning a pre-season feel to it. I receive a call from John Stern, the *Wisden Cricketer* editor, to write a piece should we win. It all seems like tempting fate. I really want the game to start now and to get stuck in.

No news on whether Tahir will be here. We are playing on a fresh wicket that looks pretty cracked, very similar to the Lancashire wicket, to which it is adjacent. That one drew the interest of the pitch inspector. The thought of winning the game but having points docked for a substandard wicket doesn't bear thinking about!

I'm hoping that it's going to be one of those pitches that plays perfectly well despite the way it looks. And that Lancashire wicket played well enough for us to win and bat with relative comfort on the last day.

We are unchanged, unsurprisingly. Darren's groin seems OK (he had a scare of another sort a couple of days ago when burglars broke into his house at 2 a.m.) and there are no other injuries.

The verdict on my shoulder is that I will have it operated on in a couple of weeks. It's disappointing but I have to admit that it does feel a bit odd, very loose in the joint, and that at the gym I'm only operating at 50%.

Wednesday 24 September

Trent Bridge, County Championship – Day One
Hampshire 199 for nine

Taunton: Somerset 202, Lancashire 56-4
Canterbury: Kent 190-9 versus Durham

There was some consternation on the faces of the captains and TV commentators at the toss this morning. The wicket was dry, slightly cracked. Above there was dank, cheerless cloud. Do you bat first at a ground where bowling first has been the winning formula all year, or buck the trend on the assumption the wicket will deteriorate? I'm glad we won the toss and bowled, but Chris said he was unsure what to do as the coin went up. I could be wrong, but this year the wickets haves sometimes looked worse than they have played, and it's always been hard work on the first day to bat. I also think we want our bowlers, the most consistent attack in the country, to kick us off in this crucial game.

And that trend has continued. Despite a relatively solid opening partnership of 46 and a seventh wicket partnership of 55 between Dimitri Mascarenhas and Nic Pothas, we are in a very good position at the end of day one. The bowlers were exemplary in their lines and lengths, and even when we weren't taking wickets they were not scoring very quickly.

Hampshire are a difficult side to bowl at in some ways as their best player, Pothas, comes in at six and one of the most destructive batters, Mascarenhas, is in at eight. So you have to work hard to get the initial wickets but then have a task on your hands to get out their potentially most challenging players.

The wickets were shared between Darren, Charlie and Andre, with Mark picking up the first one. And it was hard going, the wicket was slow with very little carry for the seamers. A slight concern is that the dry nature of the wicket plays into the hands of Imran Tahir, their not-so-surprise pick for this game. But there has been very little evidence of spin so far, albeit it's only day one.

In the other games Somerset failed to pick up all their batting points, playing on a green seamer at Taunton. They have clearly decided to produce a result-inducing wicket so there is every chance that they will pull off a win. Durham are in a strong position against Kent, on the back of four wickets from Steve Harmison. So we are being chased hard, a slip up will probably be pounced on. Day one has been a good day; if day two goes the same way, we could be almost there.

Thursday 25 September

Trent Bridge, County Championship – Day Two
Hampshire 203 all out (Shreck 4-48) & 102 for one
Nottinghamshire 211 all out (Patel 70, Prince 57, Wagh 29)

Taunton: Somerset 202 & 66-2, Lancashire 248
Canterbury: Kent 225, Durham 289-6

I slept well last night and got to the ground looking forward to batting. We had a game of football and a bit of a stretch, then throw downs and some fielding. As regular and mundane as our pre-match routine was, everyone knew what was riding on the day's play. Would we revisit our batting frailties, or could we nail a good solid performance and put everyone at ease?

Charlie got the final wicket without too much fuss in the second over of the day. Perfect start, now the batting. Billy and Will opened up against Mascarenhas and Tremlett. The commentators have spoken more about the pitch than any other topic but, apart from keeping a little low, the ball behaved as expected. Billy was lbw early on. I strapped on my arm guard, pulled on my helmet and gloves to a chorus of good wishes.

There's always that uncertainty in the back of my mind about how I will play the first few balls: the various ways I can get out, the technical deficiencies that I could show but, as I walked out, I came back to that mantra that has served me well the last couple of years – trust yourself. My first ball from Tremlett jagged away off the seam from straight and hit me on the back hip. So I need to played dead straight, even for those balls that I think may be going leg side.

At the other end Mascarenhas is bowling straight and wobbling it around. For the first few overs I find it difficult to get my rhythm right against him, telling myself to play the line of the ball. Lbw is a real threat from Dimi, so playing the line and not getting the pad in the way is crucial. I start to feel 'in', lining the ball up nicely against Tremlett and feeling in control at the other end.

Tomlinson, the left-armer who has taken 60-odd wickets, is next into the attack, and his first few overs bring a flurry of boundaries. We are up to 56, when he gets one to straighten which hits my pads and I'm given out. My initial reaction is that I've trapped it between bat and pad but, as I walk off and think it through, I realise that it hit my pad first. I'm completely gutted when I look up to the board to see I've got 29; I felt really good and should have posted a big one. But that is the way it goes at TB, there is always a chance that you could go at any stage. That's not to say it was treacherous, far from it, but that a bowler is never out of contention, especially when the ball is relatively new.

I get back into the changing room to see that the ball had pitched just outside leg. When Will is out a couple of overs later, there is a bit of tension. But a boundary-laden stand of 116 between Samit and Ashwell bestills those beating hearts. Samit brings up his fifty off only 42 balls and including 12 fours, a perfect illustration of his batting this year. But to his deep frustration, on 70 and in no danger at all, he chips a regular ball from Tomlinson to mid-off.

What a difference an hour can make. Graeme follows next, done with some extra bounce from Tahir. 183 for five, and the game is in the balance. Chris nicks one from Tomlinson, around the wicket, to make it 192 for six. We just need a good partnership and a lead.

Instead more wickets, all out 211, an extraordinary collapse from 172 for three. Tahir took four for 55 and ran through our lower order. Ominously he spun his googly a long way.

In reply there was very little for our bowlers. The wicket looked as flat as the proverbial pancake. There was no seam movement, no swing and very little bounce. Even our spinners didn't find much assistance: it seems only Tahir looks dangerous.

So where are we at the end of day two? It looks like Somerset and Lancashire are in a tussle, whilst Durham are in an excellent position against Kent. It's an unbelievable Championship week, every team (except Hampshire) are playing either to win or to avoid relegation. We have to hope that Lancashire and Kent do us a considerable favour, given the position we find ourselves in. In the dressing room at the end, I chatted to Mark about our position. We were fairly downbeat. Let's hope tomorrow brings some good fortune.

Friday 26 September

Trent Bridge, County Championship – Day Three
Hampshire 203 & 376 for five
Nottinghamshire 211 all out

Taunton: Somerset 202 & 227, Lancashire 248 & 122 -0
Canterbury: Kent 225 & 159-5, Durham 500-8 dec

There was fog over the ground this morning, pushing back the start to 11.15. We were hopeful that the moisture in the air would translate to some movement off the pitch. And for the first session it seemed to help. The bowlers, Charlie and Andre, steamed in but we could only prise out one wicket. After lunch the sun came out, and we were condemned to toiling in the field as Nic Pothas constructed an excellent century without any trouble at all.

We are now in a terrible position. From 2.30 p.m. yesterday, everything has gone wrong. There was an air of resignation this evening. There was even the suggestion, which made sense as we thought about it, that they would bat on in the morning, knowing that whatever they set us we have to try to get.

It's ironic that our season, powered by our potent seam attack is finishing on this note. The ball is barely getting above shin height, and the ferocity of our attack resembles a chihuahua rather than the rottweiler it has been.

It looks like Durham are closing in on a win, whilst Somerset are losing. So worst-case scenario looks like a second place.

Saturday 27 September

Trent Bridge, County Championship – Day Four
Hampshire 203 & 449 for five, declared
Nottinghamshire 211 & 238 all out (Patel 77, Wagh 0)
Hampshire won by 203 runs

Taunton: Somerset 202 & 227 lost to Lancashire 248 & 183-2 by eight wickets
Canterbury: Kent 225 & 204 lost to Durham 500-8d by an innings & 71 runs

I felt utterly spent when I came off the field this afternoon. Set a virtually impossible 442 runs to win in 76 overs, we unsurprisingly fell away. Durham had bowled out Kent so we knew we had to win to take the title.

The hour's play in the morning involved Pothas and Dawson gently knocking the ball around, taking up time to ensure that our chase would be as short as possible. The cricket was so dire that it drew shouts of "get on with it" not only from the crowd but from one of the cameramen! It was pretty humiliating to have our efforts reduced effectively to being ball boys, just throwing the ball back when it came, so helpless was our position.

When it came to our run chase, we threw Graeme in to have a go. It worked for a couple of overs, but really it was gesture and no more. Thinking about it now, I'm not too surprised I got 0. I wasn't clear in my mind what I was going to do as I walked out to bat. That said, I think I would have probably got out to that ball anyway, pitching in the dangerous 'corridor of uncertainty' outside off stump and slightly holding its line.

I walked into the changing room and sat down in my seat next to Mark. I just stared out towards the wicket, still fully padded up, helmet on, holding my bat. All the tentative hopes of the last week lay in ruins, and it felt for those few moments as though the efforts of the whole season counted for nothing. I just wanted to curl up into a ball and go to sleep.

I've mentioned how a result in cricket can be seen coming from a long way off. Our probable failure in this Championship race was heralded at the end of the second day, when we had collapsed and they were 100 for one. So this afternoon was just confirmation of what we had known for a while. As a result, the atmosphere was one of deflation and disappointment, but the raw feelings had been slowly released over the last couple of days.

Once the game finished and the handshakes completed, our President Bill Russell and Mick both said a few words. Bill thanked the team for providing plenty of entertainment (!) and for coming so close. Mick echoed those thoughts but said that we weren't quite good enough so will have to improve next year. Then it was time to crack open the beers and send off season 2008 in style.

The season

County Championship – Division One

Canterbury	Kent	52		Won by 10 wickets
Headingley	Yorkshire	56		Drawn
Trent Bridge	Kent	42	21	Lost by 3 wickets
Trent Bridge	Lancashire	55	43*	Won by 7 wickets
Trent Bridge	Sussex	54	8	Lost by 73 runs
Old Trafford	Lancashire	94	0	Drawn
Southampton	Hampshire	66	67	Won by 6 wickets
Trent Bridge	Surrey	3	19	Drawn
Trent Bridge	Yorkshire	33	60	Won by 112 runs
Trent Bridge	Durham	2		Drawn
Taunton	Somerset	46	13	Drawn
Chester-le-Street	Durham	-		Abandoned, no play
Hove	Sussex	128		Drawn
Trent Bridge	Somerset	1*		Drawn
The Oval	Surrey	141		Won by inns & 143 runs
Trent Bridge	Hampshire	29	0	Lost by 203 runs

M	Inn	NO	HS	Runs	Average	100s	50s
15	24	2	143	1033	46.95	2	8

	P	W	L	D	Pts
Durham	16	6	3	7	190
Nottinghamshire	16	5	3	8	182
Hampshire	16	5	4	7	178
Somerset	16	3	2	11	174
Lancashire	16	5	2	9	170
Sussex	16	2	2	12	159
Yorkshire	16	2	5	9	159
Kent	16	4	6	6	154
Surrey	16	-	5	11	124

Friends Provident Trophy
Midland Group

Edgbaston	Warwickshire	-	Abandoned
Dublin	Ireland	0	Won by 56 runs
Trent Bridge	Northamptonshire	26	Won by 6 wickets
Trent Bridge	Leicestershire	37	Won by 2 wickets
Trent Bridge	Warwickshire	18	Lost by 52 runs
Northampton	Northamptonshire	-	Abandoned
Trent Bridge	Ireland	10	Won by 1 run
Oakham	Leicestershire	11	Lost by 13 runs

Quarter Final

Chester-le-Street	Durham	3	Lost by 1 wicket

M	Inn	NO	HS	Runs	Average	100s	50s
7	7	-	37	105	15.00	-	-

Pro-40 League – Division One

Worcester	Worcestershire	7	Won by 6 wickets
Trent Bridge	Hampshire	2	Won by 31 runs
Cheltenham	Gloucestershire	28	Won by 9 runs
Taunton	Somerset	34	Lost by 3 wickets
Trent Bridge	Durham	50*	Lost by 6 runs
Lord's	Middlesex	1	Won by 19 runs
Trent Bridge	Lancashire	9	Lost by 1 run
Trent Bridge	Sussex	8	Lost by 2 wickets

M	Inn	NO	HS	Runs	Average	100s	50s
8	8	1	50*	139	19.86	-	1

	P	W	T	L	NR	Pts
Sussex	8	5	-	1	2	12
Hampshire	8	4	-	2	2	10
Durham	8	4	-	3	1	9
Nottinghamshire	8	4	-	4	-	8
Gloucestershire	8	3	-	3	2	8
Somerset	8	3	1	4	-	7
Worcestershire	8	2	1	3	2	7
Lancashire	8	1	-	3	4	6
Middlesex	8	2	-	5	1	3

Chapter Thirteen

It is over

We were close. Given that we were favourites for relegation at the start of the year, a second-place finish is something with which to be pleased. Of course, that doesn't even come close to the actual emotions any of us were feeling on that final Saturday. It felt like a loss, and there was no consolation in being runners-up. All that effort, over the course of a long season, for so little. The game at Taunton, when we were on track to win before the rain came in, will be rued for some time to come.

Charlie Shreck won the club's Player of the Year award, a fair reflection on his superb contribution this year. I think Samit can feel slightly aggrieved as he was a cat's whisker away from winning the national award. Graeme was also pivotal in so many games with both bat and ball. Darren's season has been well documented – Mick says signing him was the most important moment of the summer. He looked a little weary towards the end. He's already flown off to start the Aussie season, and it will be interesting to see how he shapes up when he comes back to us next year.

One of the really encouraging signs for next year is that, apart from those just mentioned, the rest of us have a lot more to offer. If we had all performed as well as we could, or thereabouts, and still only managed to finish second, it would be slightly concerning. But that's not the case – we were a long way off maximum output.

Thinking back to that first game in the freezing conditions down in Canterbury, in some ways it seems like an age ago and in others just yesterday. So much has happened, so much effort and emotion spent. My overall feeling about my season is one of disappointment. On a personal note, my 1,000 championship runs is something that I will be very proud of, although I'm slightly miffed that I didn't average over 50 – that last game leaving me short. I am also proud of the way in which I overcame some pretty intense setbacks to produce some good performances. There were times when uncertainty, dread even, was at the front of my mind, yet I managed to triumph over this. As for my mid-season goals, I didn't win the Player of the Year, but I did finish in the top five batsmen.

I feel strongly about my failure to score sizeable one-day runs and about my fielding. I don't want to feel handicapped in the field again. I am going to ensure that I spend more time practising my fielding than anything else. It's frustrating that I am going to have to spend four months just getting my shoulder working when I could be using that time to improve my fielding skills, but there is very little I can do about that.

On my one-day form, I'm not exactly sure what I'm going to do. Last year, when I performed much better in the shortened version, I was less concerned with scoring runs, just occupying the crease and the runs seemed to flow. This year, that hasn't been the case, and I think I probably didn't give myself the chance to get in properly. There was definitely a difference in my mentality when I went to the wicket in four-day cricket. I have to find a method to marry together the need to score at a reasonable rate with my usual batting approach.

When I turned thirty, I said to myself that I could live with the aging process if, during the preceding year, I had grown as an individual or accomplished something. Being a year older without having taken full advantage of that time was a waste. So how does an audit of my 32nd year look?

The lack of silverware is a black mark. I have no doubt in my mind that this Nottinghamshire team is coming to a peak in terms of talent and experience. So not only is a trophy-less season a disappointment in itself, it is also a failure to realise this tremendous potential.

What about personal development? At the start of this diary I wrote about the idea of challenge: putting oneself in positions where we don't know how we will respond. There were many instances of this, mini-battles against either myself or the opposition. I wasn't perfect in my response every time, but I think I learned that more often that not I will come through successfully. The midseason Twenty20 campaign was a difficult time, and I learned that I am resilient in ways I hadn't realised. It's a good reminder that adversity is the greatest teacher.

Assuming that there will be similarly challenging times in the future, I want to remember this point and embrace whatever is thrown at me. Appreciate the whole of experience, investigate every nook and cranny of a situation, whether seemingly good or bad.

The diary-writing process itself has been an education. There have been some days when the requirement to record events has been particularly unwelcome. But, for the vast majority of time, I have enjoyed the process tremendously. I'm not sure if it has had an impact on my cricketing performance, either beneficial or otherwise.

This diary has highlighted how for me the negative emotions can be more impactful: the feelings associated with failure seem to be more intense than those of success. I'm not sure if that is a reflection of my character or the season, perhaps both, but it's made me realise that I should be a bit gentler on myself. Descending, briefly, into some lay psychology, I think I have always used failure to motivate myself, so intensifying its emotional impact to drive me forwards. But it can be difficult to live with, so a slightly softer self-assessment might not be too unwelcome.

I have had some wonderful and varied experiences from Uganda to Portofino. Sometimes the richness of experience can pass by unnoticed and with it the chance to appreciate quite what a life we lead. My year has provided me with some emotionally challenging times – and some wonderful memories as well.

My move to Nottingham is proving to have been an excellent decision. I am forever grateful for the support and acceptance that I receive from management and team-mates. Being appreciated for who you are, foibles and all, is good fortune itself.

County championship

Division One batsmen scoring 1,000 runs

	M	I	NO	HS	Runs	Ave	100	50
MR Ramprakash	14	23	3	200*	1235	61.75	6	1
MW Goodwin	16	25	2	184	1343	58.39	6	5
JA Rudolph	16	24	1	155	1292	56.17	5	6
M van Jaarsveld	16	27	3	133	1150	47.91	4	7
MA Wagh	15	24	2	141	1033	46.95	2	8
ME Trescothick	16	28	1	158	1258	46.59	3	8
MJ Di Venuto	15	27	4	184	1058	46.00	2	7
ID Blackwell	16	24	1	158	1006	43.73	3	7
JL Langer	15	26	1	188	1083	43.32	3	7
SA Newman	15	25	-	129	1044	41.76	2	8

Nottinghamshire – county championship averages

Batting

	M	I	NO	HS	Runs	Ave	100	50	ct	st
SR Patel	13	21	3	135	970	53.88	2	7	7	
MA Wagh	15	24	2	141	1033	46.95	2	8	3	
CMW Read	15	20	4	142	673	42.06	1	4	52	2
BM Shafayat	9	14	2	118	476	39.66	2	1	7	
GP Swann	12	15	1	82	523	37.35	-	4	15	
AC Voges	11	19	3	69*	550	34.37	-	3	11	
AG Prince	4	4	-	57	123	30.75	-	1	1	
MJ Wood	13	20	1	98	524	27.57	-	4	4	
PJ Franks	7	11	2	52	245	27.22	-	1	5	
MA Ealham	14	17	1	130*	329	20.56	1	-	9	
SCJ Broad	3	4	-	53	77	19.25	-	1	1	
WI Jefferson	12	20	1	80	344	18.10	-	1	18	
AR Adams	8	11	1	58	133	13.30	-	1	4	
DJ Pattinson	12	12	-	33	118	9.83	-	-	1	
RJ Sidebottom	2	3	1	11*	13	6.50	-	-	-	
CE Shreck	15	17	11	3*	9	1.50	-	-	6	
RS Ferley	1	1	1	26*	26	-	-	-	1	
AD Hales	1	-	-	-	-	-	-	-	-	

Bowling

	Overs	Mdns	Runs	Wkts	BB	Ave	5wi	10wm
AC Voges	13	4	25	3	3-21	8.33	-	
AR Adams	230.4	64	594	31	4-39	19.16	-	
RJ Sidebottom	87	26	208	10	5-55	20.80	1	
SCJ Broad	101.2	26	337	16	4-39	21.06	-	
DJ Pattinson	356.1	80	1159	47	6-30	24.65	4	
GP Swann	306.5	59	793	30	4-25	26.43	-	
CE Shreck	572.3	147	1663	58	5-40	28.67	2	
MA Ealham	362.4	102	887	30	7-59	29.56	1	1
SR Patel	167.3	38	449	12	2-26	37.41	-	
PJ Franks	156	30	573	12	2-25	47.75	-	
RS Ferley	55.1	9	136	2	1-60	68.00	-	
BM Shafayat	17	1	59	-	-	-	-	
MA Wagh	7	4	11	-	-	-	-	
AG Prince	7	-	38	-	-	-	-	
CMW Read	4	-	20	-	-	-	-	

Index

Fairfield Books

Fairfield Books is a specialist publisher of cricket books. Its aim is always to produce well-written, well-presented books that are enjoyable to read.

It has won a number of awards including *Wisden Book of the Year* (twice), *Cricket Society Book of the Year* and the *National Sporting Club Cricket Book of the Year*.

The following titles are currently in print:

Mark Wagh, *Pavilion to Crease ... and Back*

Patrick Murphy, *The Centurions – From Grace to Ramprakash*

John Barclay, *Life beyond the Airing Cupboard*

Stephen Chalke, *The Way It Was – Glimpses of English Cricket's Past*

Simon Lister, *Supercat – The Authorised Biography of Clive Lloyd*

Stephen Chalke, *Tom Cartwright – The Flame Still Burns*

Peter Walker, *It's Not Just Cricket*

Stephen Chalke, *No Coward Soul – The Remarkable Story of Bob Appleyard*

Douglas Miller, *Charles Palmer – More than just a Gentleman*

Stephen Chalke, *Runs in the Memory – County Cricket in the 1950s*

Stephen Chalke, *Ken Taylor – Drawn to Sport*

Stephen Chalke, *Five Five Five – Holmes and Sutcliffe in 1932*

David Foot, *Fragments of Idolatry – From 'Crusoe' to Kid Berg*

Stephen Chalke, *Guess My Story – The Life and Opinions of Keith Andrew*

The following titles are out of print but may be possible to track down:

John Barclay, *The Appeal of the Championship – Sussex in the Summer of 1981*

Stephen Chalke, *One More Run – with Bryan 'Bomber' Wells*

David Foot, *Harold Gimblett, Tormented Genius of Cricket*

Stephen Chalke, *At the Heart of English Cricket – Geoffrey Howard*

David Foot & Ivan Ponting, *Sixty Summers – Somerset Cricket since the War*

Stephen Chalke, *Caught in the Memory – County Cricket in the 1960s*

Douglas Miller, *Born to Bowl – The Life and Times of Don Shepherd*

Stephen Chalke, *A Summer of Plenty – George Herbert Hirst in 1906*

If you would like more details of any of these,
or would like to placed on the mailing list for future publications,
please contact:
Fairfield Books, 17 George's Road, Bath BA1 6EY
telephone 01225-335813